TEACHER EDUCATORS

Their Academic and Professional Profile

TEACHER EDUCATORS

Their Academic and Professional Profile

DR. SUSANDHYA MOHANTY
Principal, District Institute of Education and Training (DIET), Dhenkanal

Foreword by

PROF. (DR.) JAGANNATH MOHANTY
Emeritus Fellow, Ravenshaw University, Cuttack

DEEP & DEEP PUBLICATIONS PVT. LTD.
F-159, Rajouri Garden, New Delhi-110027

TEACHER EDUCATORS

ISBN 978-81-8450-315-9

Typeset by S.S. COMPOSERS
3190, Mohindra Park, Shakur Basti, Delhi-110034.

Printed in India at MAYUR ENTERPRISES
WZ Plot No. 3, Gujjar Market, Tihar Village, New Delhi-110018.

Published by DEEP & DEEP PUBLICATIONS PVT. LTD.
F-159, Rajouri Garden, New Delhi-110027.
Phones: 25435369, 25440916
E-mail: ddpbooks@yahoo.co.in • ddpubs@gmail.com
Showroom:
2/13, Ansari Road, Daryaganj, New Delhi-110002 • Telefax: 23245122

Contents

Foreword

I am extremely happy to write a foreword to this book entitled "Teacher Educators: Their Academic and Professional Profile." Dr. Susandhya Mohanty worked under my guidance for a D.Litt. degree from the Sambalpur University, Sambalpur (Orissa) in the field of Teacher Education. I am immensely impressed with her hard work and sincere effort in research activities. This book deals with academic and professional background of Teacher Educators working for Teacher Education improvement. In Chapter 1, a detailed discussion has been made on theoretical perspectives of Teacher education with special reference to its aims and objectives, pre-service and in-service Teacher education including various modes of teacher education. In Chapter 2, the writer has dealt with the historical perspectives. This work is mainly a by-product of her study on Teacher Education. She has discussed comprehensively Demographic, Academic and Professional characteristics of Teacher Educators, working in the State of Orissa at the Elementary Level. The findings of the study she has conducted, throw light on various aspects of Teacher Education in the State. The suggestions given in this work on the basis of her findings are quite enlightening and useful for solving many problems and issues standing in the way in the field of management and development of Teacher Education.

This book will no doubt, help the Teachers, Teacher Educators and Researchers and I hope it will be well received by the educationists and educational administrators in the field. Shri G.S. Bhatia, Managing Director, Deep & Deep

Publications, New Delhi evinced keen interest in bringing out this book as soon as possible. I thank for his professional gesture.

PROF. (DR.) JAGANNATH MOHANTY

Acknowledgements

I express deep and immense sense of gratitude to my guide Prof. (Dr.) Jagannath Mohanty, Emeritus Fellow, Ravenshaw (Autonomous) College, Cuttack, Prof. of Education and Former Principal, Radhanath IASE, Cuttack, for his indispensable guidance, supervision and encouragement to complete this work.

I am very much indebted Prof. (Dr.) P.C. Mohapatra, Ex-Director, SCERT (Orissa), and Prof. (Dr.) S.L. Jena, Director, SCERT (Orissa), Bhubaneswar for their impeccable advice and great encouragement for completing the work.

I pay my heartfelt gratitude to Mr. K.C. Rath (OES-I), Principal, DIET, Dhenkanal for his constant inspiration in materialising this work.

I wish to express my special gratitude to Prof. (Dr.) S. Tripathy, Director, SCERT (Orissa), Dr. C. Sahoo, Reader, Dr. PM IASE, Sambalpur and Dr. T.K. Gaya, Senior Lecturer, Dr. PM IASE, Sambalpur, who provided necessary academic assistance to me.

Many many thanks to all the Principals and Teacher Educators of DIET and S.T. Schools of Orissa who responded to my request for providing necessary data.

I am highly indebted to my father Sj. Jagannath Mohanty, mother Smt. Pusparani Mohanty and my well-wisher Smt. Allhadmohini Mohanty who cared and shared all my ideas and ideals in completing this work.

I also thank Mr. Ashok Kumar Swain, Proprietor of Maa Saral D.T.P. Centre for their timely support in bringing out this work.

DR. SUSANDHYA MOHANTY

Abbreviations

AIPSN	:	All India People's Science Network
AIR	:	All India Radio
B.A	:	Bachelor in Arts
B.D.O	:	Block Development Officer
B.Ed	:	Bachelor of Education
BGBS	:	Bharat Gyan Bigyan Samiti
B.P.Ed	:	Bachelor in Physical Education
BRG	:	Block Resource Group
B.Sc	:	Bachelor of Science
BSE	:	Board of Secondary Education
BT	:	Bachelor of Teaching
CBSE	:	Central Board of Secondary Education
CDPO	:	Child Development Programme Officer
CI	:	Circle Inspector of Schools
CMDE	:	Curriculum Material Development and Evaluation.
C.P.Ed.	:	Certificate in Physical Education
CTE	:	College of Teacher Education
DEP	:	Distance Education Programme
DI	:	District Inspector of Schools
DIET	:	District Institute of Education and Training
D.Litt.	:	Doctor of Literature
DPEP	:	District Primary Education Programme
DRU	:	District Resource Unit
ECCE	:	Early Childhood Education and Care
EFA	:	Education For All
ET	:	Educational Technology
ETEP	:	Elementary Teacher Education Programme
ETTI	:	Elementary Teacher Training Institute

EVS : Environmental Science
IAPE : Indian Association of Pre-school Education
IASE : Institute of Advanced Study in Education
IFIC : In-service Programme, Field Interaction and Innovation Co-ordination
IGNOU : Indira Gandhi National Open University
INSET : In-service Teacher Education
M.A. : Master in Arts
MHRD : Ministry of Human Resources Development.
MLL : Minimum Levels of Learning
M.Phil.. : Master in Philosophy.
M.Sc. : Master in Science
NCC : National Cadet Crop
NCERT : National Council of Educational Research and Training
NCTE : National Council of Teacher Education
NFE : Non Formal Education
NIEPA : National Institute of Educational Planning and Administration.
NPE : National Policy on Education
NSS : National Social Service
OBC : Other Backward Class
PGCE : Post Graduate Certificate in Education
PGDHE : Post Graduate Diploma in Higher Education
Ph.D. : Doctor of Philosophy
POA : Programme of Action
PSTE : Pre-Service Teacher Education
SC : Scheduled Castes
SCERT : State Institute of Educational Research and Training
SD : Standard Deviation
SI : Sub-Inspector of School
SIE : State Institute of Education
SOPT : Special Orientation for Primary School Teachers.
SRC : State Resource Centre
ST : Scheduled Tribes
STS : Secondary Training Schools
SUPW : Social Useful Productive Work
TE : Teacher Education
TEI : Teacher Education Institution

TLM : Teaching Learning Material
TV : Television
UK : United Kingdom
USA : United States of America
VEC : Village Education Committee
WE : Work Experience

Theoretical Perspectives of Teacher Education

1.1 INTRODUCTION

India's destiny is being shaped in her classrooms. In this age of science and technology, education is required to be more scientific and functional. The chief aims of national reconstruction is to raise the standard of living which depends upon the merit and standard of our school-and-college students. Education is our investment in our children, who holds the key to the future development of the country. Good school empowers pupils to compete with other students. It is recognised that education is an important corner-stone of economic growth, social development and the principal means of improving the welfare of individuals. As envisaged in the National Policy on Education, 1986 (with modification in 1992, p. 3), "Life in the coming decades is likely to bring new tensions together with unprecedented opportunities. To enable the people to benefit in the new environment, it will require a new design of human resource development. The coming generation should have the ability to internalize new ideas constantly and creatively. They have to be imbued with a strong commitment to human values and social justice. All these imply better education." Therefore, the concept of National System of Education implies that up to a given level, all students irrespective of caste, creed, location and sex should have the access to education of a comparable quality.

The National System of Education enunciates common educational structure that would be based on a National Curricular Framework which contains a common core with other components that are flexible. The common core includes the history of India's freedom movement, the Constitutional obligations and other relevant content essential to nurture national identity. These elements cut across subject areas and are designed to promote values such as India's common cultural heritage, egalitarianism, democracy and secularism, equality of sexes, protection of the environment, removal of social barriers, observation of small family norms and inculcation of scientific temper. All educational programmes will be carried on in strict conformity with secular value and peaceful co-existence. But the above mentioned objectives can only be achieved through training and imparting relevant items of knowledge and skills of teachers to be reflected in our regular class room transaction process. This enlivens the nature and quality of education in true sense of the term.

1.2 TEACHER EDUCATION *VIS-À-VIS* QUALITY OF EDUCATION

It is universally accepted that the quality of education significantly depends on the quality of teachers. A classroom offers a unique situation in which two inseparable sub-systems, namely the individual (teacher) and the group (pupils) interact in a manner, which would add new dimensions to the quality of education. Teachers play and will continue to play a crucial role in the formulation, execution and implementation of educational programmes. Therefore, they are known by various terms—cultural messengers, character-builders, social engineers, etc. and the teacher steps into the class with an intent to help his/her pupils to grow in accordance with certain predetermined goals.

The criterion of a teacher's success is the growth of his pupils towards academic and intellectual excellence, social and emotional maturity, cultural acquisitions and development of essential psychomotor abilities as well as desirable attitude, interests and appreciation. The more a teacher succeeds in enabling his pupils to grow in these directions, the more he is able to bridge the gap between the nation's aspirations and actual achievement. Thus, the teacher's performance is the most crucial in the field of education. In the words of the University Education Commission (1948), "The success of educational process depends much on the character and ability of the teacher." This view has been reinforced by the Secondary Education Commission (1952-53) by stating that "the reputation of a school and its influence on life of the community invariably depend on the kind of teacher's working on it."

The primary responsibility of the teacher is to arouse the interest of the pupils in study for which he is responsible. He is not merely to convey the factual information, the principles and the precepts, but also to stimulate the spirit of inquiry and critical thinking so that she/he may acquire the habit of exercising independent and unbiased judgment and learn to discriminate between the adequate and inadequate, relevant and irrelevant data and to avoid the extremes in haste and indecision in arriving at conclusions. No teacher who is not a master of the field, who is not in touch with the latest development in his subject and he who has not developed an untrammeled mind will ever succeed in inspiring youth with that love of truth and knowledge which is the principal objective of all education. So NPE (1986) recommended that the Government and the community should endeavour to create conditions which would help to motivate and inspire teachers on constructive and creative lines. Teachers should have the freedom to innovate, to devise appropriate methods of communication and activities relevant to the needs and capabilities of pupils, and the concerns of the community.

Standards in education are primarily determined by the quality, competence and character of teachers. It is, therefore, necessary to make a sustained effort to attract to the teaching profession a good number of talented and qualified young men and women, who leave the schools and Universities every year and to retain them as dedicated, enthusiastic and contented teachers. While analyzing the important role of teachers, The National Commission on Teachers (1983-85) emphasized that the formation of character in response to the national goals, would constitute his (teacher's) primary task. He will prepare students for examinations and open to them the world of knowledge. It could be observed that the role pattern of teacher can be fairly predicted as an Instructor and as an 'Educator'. When acting as an Instructor, the teacher is concerned mainly with conveying a predetermined body of information or set of skills, when acting as educator he is concerned primarily with care, welfare and development of the individual pupil because teaching in true sense is not mere instruction but influence.

The teacher's duty is not merely to communicate knowledge in specific subjects but also to help children grow in their fullest stature, develop suitable attitude and unfold their personality. The role of teacher is synonymous with that of a catalytic agent which accelerates the interaction between two sub-systems, namely, the pupils and the educational content. The catalytic-role-playing-behaviour of a teacher is, however, governed by two considerations his personality characteristic and his ability to communicate with his pupils. Sorensen and Husk (1963) in their attempt to analyze the teacher's role specified six dimensions. They are information giver, disciplinarian, advisor, counselor, motivator and referee. Qualitative improvement in education depends on proper training of teachers. Unless the teacher is influenced by some other elements, she/he follows the same system of teaching which she/he is familiar with. But today under the changed circumstances, there is a great need for adopting new and progressive system.

1.3 MEANING OF TEACHER EDUCATION

According to the Good's Dictionary of Education (1959, p. 550) "Teacher Education means all the formal and informal activities and experiences that help to qualify a person to assume the responsibilities of a member of the educational profession or to discharge his responsibilities more effectively or the program of activities and experiences developed by an institution responsible for the preparation and growth of persons preparing themselves for educational work or engaging in the work of the educational profession."

According to the International Encyclopedia of Teaching and Teacher-Education (1987, P. 77) "Teacher education or teacher development can be considered in three phases: pre-service, induction and in-service. The three phases are now considered as parts of a continuous process."

It has been rightly observed that while the education of professionals like medical doctors, engineers and agronomists is to a great extent basically similar all over the world, the nature of teacher education, often limited to teacher training, is strongly dependent on the level of economic development and the social context. Furthermore, it is deeply influenced by the local culture and history. That is why, one can find in the contemporary world the full range of institutionalized teacher education schemes or programs that developed throughout the history of humankind, from no specific preparation at all to sophisticated university education.

According to the Education Commission (1964-66, p. 46), "The different factors which influence the quality of education and its contribution to national development, the quality, competence and character of teachers are undoubtedly the most significant. Nothing is more important than securing a sufficient supply of high quality recruits to the teaching profession, providing them with the best possible professional preparation and creating satisfactory conditions of work in which they can be fully effective. In view of the rapid expansion of educational facilities expected during the next three plans and specially in view of the urgent need to raise standards to the highest level and to keep them continually improving these problems have now acquired unprecedented importance and urgency."

According to the Report (*ibid.*, p. 67), "A sound programme of professional education of teachers is essential for the qualitative improvement of education. Investment in teacher education yields very rich dividends because the financial resources required are small when measured against the resulting improvements in the education of millions." In the absence of other influences, a teacher tries to teach in the way in which he himself was taught by his favourite teachers and thus tends to perpetuate the traditional methods of teaching. In a situation like the present when new and dynamic methods of instruction are needed such an attitude becomes an obstacle to progress. It can be modified only by effective professional education which will initiate the teachers to the needed revolution in teaching and lay the foundation for their future professional growth. First rate teacher training institutions can thus play a crucial role in the development of education.

Teacher Education is not only meant for teaching the teacher, how to teach but also to kindle his initiative, to keep it alive, to minimize the evils of the "hits and miss" process and to save time, energy and money of the teacher and the taught. The necessity of the teacher is to perceive that the course in teacher education would help him to minimize his trouble and to appreciate that it would save the children from much of the painful process through which he has himself passed. Teacher education is needed for developing a purpose and for formation of a positive attitude for the profession.

In recent years, terms related to educational and professional preparation of teachers have been replaced by new ones in order to appropriately convey the changed meaning, function and view points. The very concept of the teacher who was taken as an agent to pass on certain information to children has undergone a change. Now, she/he is an educator who assists them for going through the process of education. The term "training" is out-dated and has been replaced by the term "education." Now training is considered as an unsuitable term, used to teach tricks to animals. Now, there is a belief that an effective teacher should possess desirable traits and insight into the overall process of education besides some tricks of the trade. The degree given at the end of Teacher Education Course is called Bachelor of Education (B.Ed.) instead of Bachelor of Teaching (BT). The term 'Teacher Education' (TE) has replaced the term

'Teacher Training" and the institution imparting such an education is called "Teacher Education Institution", (TEI), "School of Education", etc. instead of "Teacher's Training College." The Graduate student under TE was formerly considered as 'Trainee' or 'Pupil-teacher'. Now, she/he has been designated as 'Student-teacher' who is professionally motivated and more skillful.

According to the NCTE (1998, p. 23), the Teacher Education programmes shall focus on competencies and commitment in much greater magnitude in future. Such a transformation in teacher preparation strategies would emerge only after due familiarity with and adequate appreciation of indigenous thoughts developed over the decades in India. Gradually, an indigenous approach and strategy would emanate and replace the alien practices that have remained in vogue in Teacher Education for quite sometime. In recent years (1978) a new term 'mathetics' is gaining currency to denote the transaction of learning in place of teaching. Mathetics may be defined as a science of learner's behaviour while pedagogy is the science of teacher's behaviour.

1.4 AIMS AND OBJECTIVES OF TEACHER EDUCATION

According to Jangira (1979, p. 1) the ultimate aim of Teacher Education is to prepare effective teachers who are capable of bringing desired behavioural changes in pupils under their charge to an optimal in relation to the input in terms of human energy and material resources expended in the process. Teacher education attempts, or is presumed to attempt, to meet this challenge following a few assumptions. In the first place, it is assumed that there is an adequate concept of teaching. Secondly, it is assumed that this concept of teaching can be operationalised in terms of teaching behaviour patterns invariably related to desired educational outcomes. Thirdly, it is assumed that there are certain techniques of training available, through which the requisite teaching behaviour patterns can be developed in prospective teachers to effect the desired educational outcomes. Fourhly, it is assumed that once the teaching behaviour pattern are acquired by prospective teachers during the course of their training these patterns are sustained and carried over to their assigned positions in the teaching profession till more efficient teaching behaviour patterns are discovered and mastered to effect the desired educational outcomes. Lastly, it is assumed that teacher education institutions plan and execute their programmes directed to this end.

Since the teacher has responsibility for the total development of the child and to prepare him or her as a citizen having faith in and professing democratic secular and socialistic values, his own education and training should lead to the inculcation of similar values and skills based on appropriate learning experiences. Further, a teacher in the context of the new and emerging social order, is expected to have a vision of the new society and be able to work in close relationship with the immediate community. It is, therefore, not enough that a student-teacher is equipped to meet the varied needs of pupils at school, what is further required is to lay greater emphasis on practical aspects of the various components of teacher education and especially to link the teacher education programmes with the needs of the community and the national development. In other words, an intending teacher, in addition to acquiring professional skills and attitudes so as to enable him/her to play his/her role effectively in brining about the desired social change through education.

While discussing the objectives of teacher education, we need to recognize a thorough consideration of the role of the teacher and the functions of teacher education. So the discussion has to be based on some assumptions as follows:

1. Education is a part of the social process and at the same time an integral part of the large society in which it occurs.
2. Understanding of social aspects of education contributes positively to effective teaching and other allied responsibilities.
3. Understanding of social aspects of education is achieved most effectively through the conceptual framework and enquiry strategies of the several social science disciplines.

On the basis of above and other considerations, various viewpoints regarding objectives of teacher education are discussed below:

The University Education Commission (1948-49) opined that the objectives of teacher education should be formulated, keeping in view the tasks of the teacher. The right kind of teacher is one who possesses a vivid awareness of his mission. He not only loves his subject, but also loves those whom he teaches. His success will be measured not in terms of percentage of passes alone not even by the quantity of original contribution to knowledge, howsoever important as they are, but equally through the quality of life and character of men and women whom he teaches.

The Education Commission (1964-66, p. 72) recommended for the qualitative improvement of the teacher education. They emphasized that the essence of a programme of teacher education is quality, and in its absence teacher education becomes not only a financial waste but also a source of overall deterioration in educational standards. The commission suggested that the objectives of teacher education should be formulated on the basis of some broad principles, listed as under:

1. Re-orientation of subject-knowledge
2. Vitalization of professional studies
3. Improvement in methods of teaching and evaluation
4. Improvement of student-teaching
5. Development of special course and programmes
6. Revision and improvement of curriculum

The Committee on Plan Projects (1963) of the Planning Commission studied at length the issue and problems of Teacher Education aiming at education of the whole person. So every teacher should have a deep knowledge and understanding of his subject(s) and the problems as well as concerns of the community. These cannot be acquired by rule of thumb, and very often an untrained teacher has to learn the job by an arduous and long practice during which it is impossible that young children might be exposed to irreparable harm, because the teacher has not used the skills and knowledge which she/he should have. To argue that a few teachers are born and not made, would have its counter argument that one swallow does not make a summer, and the overwhelming majority of the men and women can only become good teachers if their training programme is built on a sound foundation of the theoretical knowledge and supervised practical work. This is what a Training Institution is designed to provide but admittedly, like all Academic Institutions of the same kind, no Teacher Training Institute can produce teachers with hundred percent efficiency.

The said Committee also recommended that besides the knowledge of the subject, Teacher Education should attempt:

1. To enable the trainees to acquire the skills and techniques needed to teach young children with the help of modern knowledge of child psychology and methods of teaching.
2. To inculcate in the trainees the ideals and accepted behavioural patterns of the society in which we live and whose purposes we serve.
3. To develop in the teacher-trainees certain attitudes, values and interests in conformity with the ideals of democracy and our developing economy.

Envisaging an expanded role expectation, National Council of Teacher Education's Framework of Teacher Education, the future teacher in India should—

1. Develop Gandhian values of education, such as non-violence, truthfulness, self-discipline, self-reliance and dignity of labour.
2. Perceive his role as an agent of social change in the community.
3. Perceive his role not only as a leader of the children but also that of a guide to the community.
4. Act as a liaison between the school and the community and employ suitable ways and means

for integrating community life and resources with school work.

5. Not only use it but also helps in the conservation of environmental resources and preservation of historical monuments and other cultural heritage.
6. Possess warm and positive attitude towards growing children in their academic, socio-emotional, and personal problems and skills to guide and counsel them.
7. Develop an understanding of the objectives of school education in the Indian context and awareness of the role of the school in achieving the goals of building up a democratic, secular and socialistic society.
8. Develop understanding, interest, attitudes and skills which would enable him to foster all-round growth and development of the children under his care.
9. Develop competence to teach on the basis of the accepted principles of learning and teaching.
10. Develop communication and psychomotor skills and abilities conducive to human relations for interacting with the children in order to promote learning inside and outside the classroom.
11. Keep abreast of the latest knowledge of the subject matter he is teaching and the techniques of teaching the same.
12. Undertake action research and investigatory projects.

A more systematic approach in formulating the general objectives would be to make them explicit and to ensure that they are both logically consistent and reflect the growing professional as well as national demand confronting the teacher in school and/or in the community. A set of broad objectives which may be central to any Teacher Education Programme in India regardless of the structure and stage or level are as follows

(a) To develop concepts and acquire understanding of

those areas and aspects of knowledge which have professional significance.

(b) To develop an understanding of educational theory which will inform professional judgment and actions.

(c) To develop technical skills necessary for the achievement of professional competence.

(d) To develop understanding of the relationship between logical and psychological aspects of the teaching-learning process at a given stage of the human development.

(e) To develop skills to organize educational institutions as educational, cultural and social center for the community.

(f) To develop faith in democratic, socialistic and secular values and provide experiences and skills in organizing community living based on those values.

The Teacher Education Department of National Council of Educational Research and Training (NCERT), New Delhi after organizing in depth deliberations, seminars, meetings and workshops have evolved stage-wise objectives of Teacher Education, which are given below.

1.5 OBJECTIVES OF PRE-PRIMARY TEACHER EDUCATION

The NCERT has spelt out the following objectives of teacher education to prepare teachers for pre-primary stage.

1. To acquaint the student-teacher with the philosophy and sociology of pre-school education so that he can understand the basic principles of pre-school education and through it he can realize the needs, values and aspirations of the society.
2. To make him conversant with the growth and development of pre-school education both in India and abroad.
3. To develop in the teacher an understanding of the

principles and processes of the various aspects of children's growth and development.

4. To help the student-teacher to realize the importance of health, nutrition and welfare services for the child through proper information and to develop in him the skills to provide the same through appropriate measures.
5. To acquaint him with the methods, practices, equipment,. materials and organizational principles of pre-school education, so that he can use them effectively in his day-to-day work.
6. To develop in him and awareness of the important roles of parents and community in the education of pre-school children and to make him conversant with the ways of enlisting their help and cooperation in various programmes of the pre-school education.
7. To give him a better command over the language of everyday use and to help him understand the physical and social phenomena around him so that he can make a meaningful interpretation of the world to children under his charge.
8. To equip him with the knowledge of various media of creative self-expression and to develop in him essential skills for guiding children in the pursuit of creative arts and crafts.
9. To acquaint him with his professional obligations and rights and to develop in him a positive attitude towards his profession.
10. To inculcate in him a sense of desirability of constant professional growth.

1.6 OBJECTIVES OF TEACHER EDUCATION FOR PRIMARY STAGE

In view of the increase in the children's maturity and for attaining their main objectives of literacy, numeracy and technocracy, along with other socio-emotional objectives, special attention will have to be paid to the development of specialized knowledge and skills with regard to content and methodology. So the primary teacher trainee should:

1. Possess competence in the first and second language, Mathematics and in the topics of Natural and Social Sciences related to environment.
2. Develop skills in identifying, selecting and learning experiences for teaching the above subjects in formal and non-formal situation.
3. Possess sufficient theoretical and practical knowledge of health, physical and recreational activities, work experience, art and music and skills for conducting these activities.
4. Develop understanding the psychological principles underlying the growth and development of the children of the age group 6+ to 14+.
5. Acquire theoretical and practical knowledge about childhood education, including integral teaching.
6. Develop understanding of major learning principles which would help in promoting cognitive, psychomotor and attitudinal learning.
7. Understand the role of home, peer group and community, in shaping the personality of the child and help to develop an amicable home-school relationship for mutual benefit.
8. Conduct simple action research.
9. Understand the role of school and the teacher in changing the society.

1.7 OBJECTIVE OF TEACHER EDUCATION FOR THE SECONDARY STAGE

The Secondary teacher-trainee should:

1. Possess competence to teach subjects of his specialization on the basis of accepted principles of learning and teaching in the context of the new school curriculum.
2. Develop skills, understanding, interest and attitude which would enable him to foster all-round

growth and development of the children under his care.

3. Possess sufficient theoretical and practical knowledge of health and physical education, games and recreational activities and work experience.
4. Develop skills in identifying, selecting, innovating and organizing learning experiences for teaching the above mentioned general and special subjects.
5. Develop understanding of psychological principles of growth and development, individual differences and similarities, and cognitive psychomotor and attitudinal learning.
6. Develop skills in guiding and counseling the children in solving their personal as well as academic problems.
7. Understand the role of home, peer group and the community in shaping the personality of the child and help to develop an amicable home-school relationship for mutual benefit.
8. Understand the role of the school in changing the society.
9. Undertake investigatory projects and action research.

1.8 TYPES AND MODES OF TEACHER EDUCATION

1.8.1 Pre-service Teacher Education

According to Willey and Maddison (1971), "Sending into schools unsuitable persons, badly trained, can be as harmful to school children as any shortage of teacher." In fact, poor teaching by badly trained teachers can be more harmful than no teaching; for in the former case the child has learnt wrong things whereas in the later case he has not learnt anything wrong. Therefore, it is necessary that the minimum essential components of pre-service Teacher Education programme should be identified and implemented so that the teacher so prepared can discharge his/her complex functions satisfactorily. Taylor (1983) has observed, "Teacher Education is Janus-faced. In one direction, it faces classroom and school with their demands for relevance, practicability, competence and technique. In the other, it faces the university and the world of research, with their stress on scholarship, theoretical fruitfulness and disciplinary vigor." "The challenge is not to prove the superiority of either perspective, but to bring to the primary requirement for classroom competence an evolving body of theory, which can illuminate, facilitate and enrich that competence. At the same time, professional experience is the laboratory in which the tidy generalizations of the lecture theatre are put to the test." While the study of educational theory in the form of disciplines such as psychology, sociology, philosophy and history was considered necessary for Teacher Education, unless they are related to the practical problems faced by the classroom teacher, they do not seem relevant. As Naish and Hartnett (1975) put it, "The job of theory is to evoke judgment rather than rote obedience. The application of theory to practice is the bringing to bear critical intelligence upon practical tasks rather than the implementation of good advice."

By the mid-1070s in the UK and the USA, a systematic approach to pedagogy led to isolation of separate skills involved in the teaching process. About twenty skills of teaching, each with its own distinguishing components, were identified and teachers were trained by techniques such as micro-teaching, interaction analysis, use of audio video for self-confrontation, stimulation and role play. It was found that practicing these skills separately and then practicing the integration of the skills in the teaching-learning process produce a more effective teacher than practicing to teach without any training in skills. In India also, since mid-1970s skill-based Teacher Education is followed in many good institutions of Teacher Education. This, however, means that more time should be devoted to the practical aspects of Teacher Education. "If the skill approach to education is accepted, teacher training will require a needful and competency-based approach, evaluated by competency outcomes where young people passing through such a learning process, would be encouraged and assisted by trainers whose assumption throughout would be related to attainable goals by all rather then unassailable peaks for none except the tiny few" (Alexander, 1984). A teacher status, therefore, would send out a simple statement of the progressive achievement of competencies in a number of defined and agreed areas of personal development and their "employability" by the student, in terms of knowledge, skill and attitudes demonstrated by his or her behaviour in given situations.

Considering the importance of the practical aspects of Teacher Education, the Teacher Education Curriculum- a Frame-work, recommended by NCTE in 1978, gave a weightage of 80% to the practical and weightage of 20% to the theoretical aspects. The practical aspects include working with community. The core training programme (which is training in teaching skills), special training programme (which is training in teaching techniques related to school subjects), related practical work (which refers to practical work related to the educational theory subjects) and special training programme for health, physical education, art, music and recreational activities even in the last mentioned training programme, the trainee learns how to organize such activities in the schools.

Even in the USA supervised professional experience is given about one half of the total time for professional education. As stated by Prof. R. Freeman Butts of Columbia University, "Supervised professional experience should include observation, participation, student-teaching and competence in the methods of teaching and use of instructional materials. This aspect should comprise about one half of professional education" (Hodenfield and Stinnett, 1961)

Different structures of Teacher Education have been evolved in different countries. In the UK for pre-service Teacher Education for Primary schools, two-year certificate prevailed till 1960, between 1960 to 1970, it became a three-year certificate and thereafter, it was changed to four-year concurrent B.Ed. That is professional teacher education in giving concurrently with degree level academic subjects. For secondary education, one can have the 4 year concurrent B.Ed. or B.A./B.Sc. + Post Graduate Certificate in Education

(PGCE). The Post-Graduate Certificate in Education is a professional course in University departments of education. In the USA, the usual pattern of Teacher Education is a four-year degree course in education similar to the concurrent B.Ed. Course of the U.K.

It is, however, also possible for a Graduate in Arts or Science to obtain a teacher's certificate by taking certain required courses in professional education (usually one or two semesters). Even in the concurrent four-year degree course, the duration of professional education is approximately one year (though it is spread over four years). It has been felt that the duration of professional education should be increased.

In India, we have one year certificate course after high school certificate in some state for Primary Teacher Education. In other states, it is a two-year certificate course after high school/higher secondary school certificate. The trend is towards two-year certificate after higher secondary certificate course. The NCTE stipulates entry qualification (+2 or 12 year schooling) for the two-year Primary Teacher Training and sets a deadline (September 2005) for states with one-year programme to switch over the two-year courses. It may be desirable to try a three-year Degree course with both academic and professional subjects taught concurrently for preparing Primary Teachers. This appears to be a reasonable idea since content-base of teacher-trainees needs to be sufficiently strengthened. For preparing Secondary Teachers, we have one-year B.Ed. course after B.A/B.Sc. or the four-year integrated B.A.B.Ed./B.Sc. B.Ed. course of the Regional Colleges of Education. The four year integrated course is generally considered a better model of Teacher Education, as it gives a longer period of time for providing the student with the knowledge, skills and attitudes required for a teacher. The National Commission of Teachers 1983-85 (with Dr. Chattopadhyay as Chairman) recommended the four-year training course after Senior Secondary leading to B.A./B.Sc. and B.Ed. for preparation of teachers for Secondary Schools. Even in India, the duration of one year B.Ed. degree is often felt inadequate for imparting professional education and a two-year course has been sometimes suggested. However, on practical consideration, the two-year course has not been implemented in. It has been argued that the one year professional education if well-utilised can provide the basic competencies required for a beginning teacher and that further professional growth should be accomplished through mandatory in-service education.

1.8.2 In-Service Teacher Education

In all professions there are special course of study which an entrant has to go through, even though she/he has pre-service training and professional education. There is need for further education, in professions or trades, where methods and techniques undergo changes rapidly or where there is an explosion of knowledge. Further training for persons in training is badly required, especially, in the teaching profession, because pedagogical theory and practice are changing at a faster rate than in most other professions. Hence, every teacher needs to refresh his knowledge of theory and practice through in-service education.

The Education Commission in its report (1964-66) recommended that "There is need for the organization of a large scale, systematic and co-ordinated programme of in-service education so that every teacher would be able to receive at least two or three months of in-service education in every five years of service."

The National Commission on Teachers (1986) had recommended that " Attendance at an in-service training course be made mandatory for every teacher at least once in five years." (Revised Guidelines DIET 1994, SCERT, Orissa, p. 8)

According to the report of an Expert Committee of NCTE, 1995 "Teacher should be suitably motivated to enroll in in-service courses. The in-service course should be based on the felt needs of teachers as well as to meet their deficiencies of knowledge. At the end of the in-service course, a test should be given to evaluate the knowledge and understanding gained by the teachers and a certificate be issued on satisfactory results in the test." (*ibid.*, p. 15)

The Correspondence/Distance education is not considered appropriate for pre-service teacher education.

Therefore, the committee recommended that Correspondence/ Distance Education mode may be used for in-service teacher education of teachers at all levels who have already obtained their first degree/diploma in teacher education. It also added that all instructional materials of an in-service education course should be revised at least once in every five years so that they would incorporate latest development and waive-out obsolete knowledge. Further, as far as possible, multimedia packages in self-instructional style should be developed for In-service Education Courses. (*ibid.*, p. 15)

According to the Revised Guidelines for Programmes and Activities (SCERT, Orissa, Bhubaneswar, 1994, p. 7), the objectives of providing in-service education to teachers are as follows:

1. To provide every teacher, as far as possible, knowledge, skills and attitudes which may be necessary for him to function as a competent professional, and
2. to afford teachers' opportunities of professional growth suited to their individual background, aptitude, talent and choice.

Although the subject of School and Teacher education is looked after by the State Government, the responsibility of providing in-service education and support to school teachers is shared by a number of institutions controlled by both Government and autonomous organizations, such as NCERT (National Council of Educational Research and Training), NIEPA (National Institute of Educational Planning and Administration), SCERT (State Council of Educational Research and Training), CBSE (Central Board of Secondary Education), and the BSE (Board of Secondary Education). With reorganization and restructuring of Teacher Education since 1986, on the recommendation of the NPE (1986 and 1992), a number of institutions such as District Institutes of Education and Training (DIETs), Colleges of Teacher Education (CTEs) and Institutes of Advanced Study in Education (IASEs) are catering to the in-service training of teachers. This aside, District Primary Education Programme

(DPEP/Serva Shiksha Abhiyan (SSA), the Government of India sponsored programmes also organizes capacity building programme for working teachers.

In our State, a great deal of responsibility was given to SCERT. It has the major role of planning, organizing, sponsoring, monitoring and evaluating the in-service education programme for all levels of teachers, instructors and other educational personnel. The State level agency would take into consideration the needs of teachers, such as changing national goals, revision of school curriculum, additional inputs in teaching-learning system, etc. before preparing a programme of in-service education for a period of time.

In the district, DIET is the premier agency to conduct the programe of in-service education for primary teachers. DIETs also organize a few programmes for Headmasters, Principals and other supervisory staff like DIs (District Inspector of Schools) and SIs (Sub-inspector of Schools)

Strategies adopted for in-service teacher education programme, vary programme-wise and theme-wise. One has to judiciously select an appropriate training strategy keeping in view the theme, programme duration, background of participants, availability of resource persons, support materials and technologies of training at hand. Training strategies range from Lecture-*cum*-discussion to project work, group interaction, activity-based approach, field visit, case study, brain storming, panel discussion, etc. Over the years, there has been a perceptible shift from trainer-dominated mode to participatory/interactive mode, making the in-service training programmes more efficient and effective.

To conclude, the theoretical perspective of Teacher-Education has been stated and explained in terms of the role performance, aims and objectives, meaning and significance. In this context, the concerns and commitments of Teacher Education have been taken into account and objectives of Teacher Education at different stages, i.e. Pre-primary, Primary and Secondary have been streamlined and specifically mentioned. On the whole, Teacher Education by its very nature has been inter-disciplinary. It implies that Teacher Education programmes include economics, history and culture. It also highlights the emerging trends of mathetics in place of pedagogy with its various modes of transaction like face-to-face and open learning system. No teacher education programme can remain relevant and progressive without being resilient to the patterned and directions of development in school education. Stoic indifference and insensitiveness to change outside will inevitably lead to irrelevance and inefficiency.

2

Historical Perspectives of Teacher Education

The ancient Indian Law-giver Manu once said, "A teacher is the image of Brahma (the creator of the universe)." An old Indian prayer invokes, "The teacher is God Brahma, he is God Bishnu, he is God Maheswar. He is the whole universe, obeisance to the teacher." Thus in the Indian culture, teacher was given a higher position than parents because he opened the pupils' eyes of knowledge and moulded their character.

According to the Western culture. "A teacher affects eternity, he can never tell where his influence stops" (Adams). Henry Vyke observes, "I sing the praise of the unknown teacher, king of himself and leader of mankind." The American Commission of Teacher Education also observed that "The quality of its citizen depends not exclusively, but in a critical measure, upon the quality of their education. The quality of their education depends more than upon any single factor on the quality of their teacher" (Mohanty, 1996, p. 68).

It has been rightly pointed out by Mohanty (*ibid.*, p. 68) that the teacher is the backbone of the educational system, maker of the mankind and architect of the society. Since the status of teachers and conditions of their work have a direct bearing on the quality of education, many maladies of the society are attributed to the present system of education. Hence, various efforts have been made in the Post-Independent India for improving the quality of education, particularly Teacher Education. Evidently, Teacher Education sector has experienced impressive and unprecedented developments since Independence, more particularly with formulation of National Policy on Education and the programme of Action (1986 and 1992).

Historically viewed, the present system of Teacher Education in India and in the Indian states is at the one end of a continuous: from the Pre-Independent period, with over arching colonial designs, to Post-Independent era with dreams and visions to redesign the dysfunctional system. The present chapter is an attempt to look at the development of Teacher Education in a historical perspective.

2.1 TEACHER EDUCATION IN PRE-INDEPENDENCE ERA

In the Vedas, Upanishads, Brahmans, Purans and Epics, a teacher was held in high esteem, and character building and salvation were regarded as main aims of education. The Acharya was the highest of all teachers and was supposed to initiate pupils to the Vedas and Vedangas. In the Buddhist period, the status of Acharyas was also high; they were engaged in imparting knowledge about religion and morality. In the medieval period, although Muslims had their education in maktabs and madrasas, teachers were playing an important role not only in teaching but also in producing religious persons.

Normal school was established in Bombay for training primary teachers. Subsequently, high school teachers were trained and the training courses included both theory and practice of teaching. More and more training colleges were established throughout the country. There was rapid development of teacher education in the period from 1937 to 1947 and the number of training colleges increased from 23 to 42 while that of normal schools increased from 537 to 650 (Misra, 1993, p. 119).

The Woods Despatch of 1854 and the Despatch of 1859 emphasised the need of training of teachers and suggested that initiative had to be taken for training the vernacular and the other teachers in Normal Schools. The Report of the Indian Education Commission (1882) strongly endorsed the usefulness of the training courses for the primary and secondary teachers. The Commission also recommended to set-up more Normal Schools for training of teachers. The Government of India's Resolution on Education Policy (1904) made some significant suggestions for the improvement of teacher training programmes, like recruiting more men of ability and experience to equip the training colleges adequately, to make the duration of training programme for two years for non-graduates and one year for graduates and to make the training course more sound with theory and practice. The Resolution helped in the increase of Elementary Teacher Training Institutions in the country.

The Calcutta University Commission (1917), under the Chairmanship of Sir Micheal Sadler, laid stress on the need for increasing the number of trained teachers. It also recommended the opening of Education Department for training of teachers under the University. Practice teaching schools were attached to the training colleges and to the Education Departments. The Commission also suggested to include "Education" as one of the subjects in the Colleges and Universities. The Hartog Committee (1929) also recommended to organize Refresher courses for teachers in service so as to keep them in touch with the latest practices in education.

The National Movement for Independence included Basic Education scheme under the patronage of Mahatma Gandhi since 1937. Basic Training Schools were set-up for training of teachers. The Abbott Wood Report (1937) suggested that the Normal Schools should function themselves with the "what" as well as "how" of education. For the first time, social responsibility was given to teachers, and community work and community service found a place in Teacher Training.

The Central Advisory Board of Education (CABE) during forties considered training as essential for teachers.

Specific qualifications were fixed for teacher trainees and practice teaching was given importance.

The Sargent Report (1894) formulated a plan for improving the Education System. It made recommendations, *inter alia*, on Teacher Education which included Teacher Training at various levels, Refresher courses, visits to other schools and giving stipend to the trainees. Thus there was a trend in giving emphasis on Teacher Training both for quantitative and qualitative improvement of education.

2.2 TEACHER EDUCATION AFTER INDEPENDENCE

After Independence, education was regarded as the potential instrument of social transformation and an important means of National Development (Mohanty, 1994, p. 8). Education was required to meet the emerging demands and challenges in various fields. Reforms in education were felt urgent and a few Committees and Commissions were appointed to review the existing system and suggest measures for improvement. The reports also discussed Teacher Education and recommended steps for improving Teacher Education. Besides, some committees and work rules were formed specifically for improving Teacher Education in the country. These are briefly described as follows:

The University Education Commission (1948-49) was appointed by the Government of India under the Chairmanship of Dr. S. Radhakrishnan. Although it was expected to make recommendations for improving University Education, it also suggested different measures for improving the standard of teaching and for that purpose, training and research at the University level. The Commission felt that in our secondary schools and Colleges, educational standards were undoubtedly low and in order to improve them, we should improve our teaching. The service conditions are also to be improved. The Commission added that University standard could improve if the colleges were improved. It was for the universities to provide continuous supply of highly trained and efficient teachers for these institutions (NCTE, 1998, p. 160). For this purpose, more vacational refresher courses were to be organized for the secondary school and college teachers.

The Secondary Education Commission (1952-53) was constituted by Government of India under the Chairmanship of Dr. A. Laxmanswami Mudaliar to examine the prevailing system of Secondary Education. The major recommendations on Teacher Education suggested that teacher trainees should receive training both in curricular and extracurricular activities. The Training Colleges should not only organize pre-service training courses, but also arrange refresher courses, vacational courses, etc. for teachers. Training Colleges should also conduct research work in different aspects of pedagogy and other aspects of Teacher Education. In order to meet the shortage of women teachers, special part-time training courses should be provided (*ibid.*, p. 162).

The National Committee on Women's Education, (1958) was appointed by the Government of India under the Chairmanship of Shrimati Durgabai Deshmukh. It advised for selecting suitable candidates for training, providing hostel, holding coaching classes and part-time courses for women teachers. It also suggested for part-time employment of women teachers and for giving compulsory training in local dialect to all teachers as a part of their professional education.

Review Committee on Education was set-up by the UGC under the Chairmanship of Prof. N.K. Sidhant. The Committee examined the standards of teaching and research and suggested measures for improving them. It recommended that teaching should be supplemented by tutorials and seminars, and practice teaching should be given more emphasis.

The Study-Team appointed by the Planning Commission in 1961 under the Chairmanship of Sri B.N. Jha, recommended that every Teacher should have a deep knowledge and skill in applying the same. The training programme should be built on a sound foundation of theoretical knowledge and supervised practice teaching. As regards the objectives of Teacher Training, the following suggestions were made:

(i) To enable the trainees to require the skills and techniques needed to teach young children with the help of modern knowledge of child psychology and methods of teaching;

(ii) to inculcate in the educants the ideals of accepted behaviour patterns of the society in which they live and whose purpose they serve; and

(iii) to develop in the Teacher Trainees certain attitudes, values and interests in conformity with the ideals of democracy and our developing economy (*ibid.*, p. 174)

The Study Group on Training of Teachers in India was appointed by the Government of India under the Chairmanship of Shri Raja Ray Singh in 1961. The Group was to prepare the programme for improvement of Teacher Training at the Primary stage. It rightly observed that no other single factor could make such a vital difference for the better, as a proper system of Teacher Education and a "break-through was urgently necessary. In order to clear the backlog of untrained teachers, it suggested both short-term and long-term in-service training facilities and appointment of study groups for various aspects of teacher education. Besides in-service training programme, extension services should be provided for primary school teachers. It also suggested for establishing State Institutes of Elementary Education providing further education, producing educational literature, setting-up State Council of Teacher Education and so on.

The Education Commission (1964-66), appointed by Government of India under the Chairmanship of Prof. D.S. Kothari, reviewed the principles and policies for the development of education at all stages and in all aspects. It laid emphasis on professional preparation of teachers for qualitative improvement of education.

The Commission felt that the existing isolation of Teacher Education should be removed in the following manner:

(a) Education as distinguished from pedagogy, should be recognized as an independent academic discipline and introduced as an elective subject in courses for the first and second degree;

(b) Schools of Education should be established in selected universities in collaboration with other University disciplines to develop programmes in Teacher Education and studies and research in Education;

(c) extension work should be regarded as an essential function of Teacher Training Institutions and an Extension Service Department should be established in each training institution, Pre-primary and Secondary—as an integral part of it;

(d) effective associations of alumni should be established to bring all students and faculty together to discuss and plan curriculum;

(e) practice-teaching for teachers under training should be organized in active collaboration with selected schools which should receive recognition from the Education Department as Co-operative Schools and special grants for equipment and supervision; and

(f) periodic exchange of staff of the Co-operative Schools and Teacher Training Institutions should be arranged (*ibid.*, pp. 191-92)

For improving the quality of Teacher Education, the Commission laid stress on organization of content courses, introduction of integrated courses, using improved methods of teaching, improving practice teaching and revising curricula at all stages of Teacher Education. The Commission also recommended that some steps to be taken for improving Training Institutions both for Secondary as well as Primary teachers through staff improvement, duration increase of correspondence course and other physical facilities.

The National Policy of Education (1986) sought to implement certain recommendations of the Kothari Commission. It tried to implement certain recommendations for improving Teacher Education also. It regarded Teacher Education as a continuous process the pre-service and in-service components. It being inseparable, suggested the establishment of District Institutes of Education and Training

(DIETs) with the capability to organize pre-service and in-service courses for Elementary School Teachers. Nearly 430 DIETs have already been established by 1997-98. It required the National Council for Teacher Education (NCTE) for equipping itself, accrediting institutions of Teacher Education and to provide guidance on curricula and methods.

The Programme of Action (POA) 1992 enunciated the following functions of an Elementary Teacher Education Institutions:

(a) Pre-service and in-service education of teachers for the formal school system;
(b) induction level and continuing education of non-formal and adult education instructors and supervisors;
(c) training and orientation of heads of institutions in institutional planning and management and micro-level planning;
(d) orientation of community leaders, functionaries of voluntary organizations and other influencing school level education;
(e) academic support to school complexes and District Boards of Education;
(f) action research and experimentation work;
(g) serving as evaluation centers for primary and upper primary schools as well as non-formal and adult education programmes;
(h) provision of services of a resource and learning center for teachers and instructors; and
(i) consultancy and advice, for example, to District Boards of Education.

The NCTE estalished in 1973 performed the above mentioned functions with earnestness.

The Review Committee of NPE was formed in 1990 with Acharya Ram Murti as Chairman. The Committee's report entitled "Towards Enlightened Human Society" recommended that the training programme should be competency-based and an integration of theory and practice. In-service and Refresher course should be organized on the specific needs of teachers. Besides, innovative activities would be undertaken by the DIETs which are to develop in the respective areas enumerated below.

(a) Universalization of Elementary Education;
(b) Early Childhood Care and Education;
(c) Women's education with emphasis on giving a gender perspective to the entire educational process;
(d) Education for promoting equity and social justice among Schedule Castes, Schedule Tribes and other educationally backward sections of society, including minorities;
(e) Vocationalisation of the entire educational process; and
(f) Examination reforms, modernization, multiple entry exit points.

The Program of Action (POA, 1992) suggested some Centrally Sponsored Schemes or Teacher Education and also for strengthening SCERTs and NCTE for implementing their programmes more effectively.

The NCTE became a statutory body by Parliament (No. 73 of 1993) with a view to achieving plan and co-ordinated development of Teacher Education, regulation and proper maintenance of norms and standards in Teacher Education. The Council under this Act was required to perform its function as follows:

(a) to undertake surveys and studies relating to various aspects of Teacher Education and publish the result, thereof;
(b) to make recommendations to the Central and State Governments, Universities, University Grants Commission and recognized institutions in the matter of preparation of suitable plans and programmes in the field of Teacher Education;

(c) to co-ordinate and monitor Teacher Education and its development in the country;

(d) to lay down guidelines in respect of minimum qualification for a person to be employed as a teacher in schools or in the recognized institutions;

(e) to lay down norms for any specified category of course or training in Teacher Education, including the minimum eligibility criteria for admission thereof and the method of selection of candidates, duration of the course, course content and mode of curriculum;

(f) to lay down guidelines for compliance by recognized institutions, for starting new courses of training and for providing physical and instructional facilities, staffing pattern and staff qualifications;

(g) to lay down standards in respect of examinations leading to Teacher Education qualifications, criteria for admission to such examinations and schemes of courses or training;

(h) to lay down guidelines regarding tuition fees and other fees chargeable by recognized institutions;

(i) promote and conduct innovation and research in various areas of Teacher Education and disseminate the results thereof;

(j) to examine and review periodically the implementation of the norms, guidelines and standards laid down by the Council and to suitably advise the recognized institutions;

(k) to evolve suitable performance appraisal systems, norms and mechanisms for enforcing accountability on recognized institutions;

(l) to formulate schemes for various levels of Teacher Education and identify recognized institutions and set-up new institutions for Teacher Development Programmes,

(m) to take all necessary steps to prevent commercialization of teacher education; and

(n) to perform such other functions as may be entrusted to it by the Central Government.

The NCTE has been implementing the programmes as assigned in the Statue. The Council constituted an Expert Committee under the chairmanship of Dr. R.C. Das in 1994 to examine the reports and documents and suggest action for improving Teacher Education. The Committee recommended for consolidating the courses of Teacher Education and part-time, face-to-face and institutionalized programmes of Teacher Education. It also recommended Correspondence/ Distance education mode, to be used effectively for In-service Education. It also suggested some measures for reducing commercialization in the system to the minimum.

2.3 DEVELOPMENT OF TEACHER EDUCATION IN ORISSA BEFORE INDEPENDENCE

According to Nath (1968, p. 229) "Professional training of the teachers of Orissa did not get started until the early decade of the 19th century when the Mission School of Cuttack started a department for training teachers to Gospel (Christian) teaching. In the village school, traditional rote method was followed for forming alphabets on the dust and repeating the multiplication table in parrot-like sing-song manner were followed, which did not require any formal training."

Lord Stanley, the first Secretary of the State emphasized the training of teachers as per the recommendation of the Despatch of 1854. The first Normal School was established at Cuttack in 1869, which had two departments – one is Good Training department and another is Pundit Training department. Gradually, teacher training institutions were set-up in different parts of Orissa not only for Primary schools, but also for High schools. The first Training College at Cuttack was established in 1923 for preparing higher qualified teachers. There were Secondary Training Schools at Cuttack and Berhampur. The number of Training Schools increased from six to twenty six during the period 1884 to 1912.

During the period from 1912 to 1936 the programme of Teacher Education became popular in Bihar-Orissa. In 1930, the School Examination Board was formed for conducting examination for Elementary and Secondary Training Schools.

The Elementary Training Course was changed in 1931 in which an attempt was made to relate instruction with rural life and environment. In 1936, many institutions of different grades (Lower Elementary, Higher Elementary and Secondary Training Schools) came into existence. In South Orissa, the number of training schools were seven whereas in North Orissa it was 14 by 1936. The curriculum was mainly literary and was not child-centred.

In 1936, the province of Orissa was born on the Ist April and the Government tried to streamline the Teacher Training system in respect to curriculum, duration and so on. The training course was extended to two years in all the Secondary Training Schools. The Cuttack Training School has 30 seats and there were 25 stipends for the students. Basic Training Schools were set-up during this period. Although Teacher Training suffered a setback due to Second World War and political disturbances, the situation was changed as the Post-war scheme was implemented to improve the infrastructure of the Training Schools.

2.4 DEVELOPMENT OF TEACHER EDUCATION IN ORISSA AFTER INDEPENDENCE

By 1968, three Training Colleges were set-up in Orissa, one at Cuttack, one at Angul and another at Sambalpur. Subsequently, Regional College of Education was also established at Bhubaneswar. B.Ed. Course was available in all the Colleges and M.Ed. Course was available in Training Colleges at Cuttack and Sambalpur.

The number of Training Schools rose from three to sixty-five in the year 1978 and again it was increased to seventy in the year 1988. The number of Elementary Training Schools, similarly increased from twenty-nine to seventy-nine during the period 1961 to 1966. The Elementary Training Schools were either abolished or upgraded to Secondary Training Schools. After Independence, six Basic Training Schools were opened during 1947-49 which continued to train teachers for Primary and Basic Schools till 1969. Then, they were converted to Secondary Training Schools.

The State Institute of Education was established in 1964

for improving the quality of Elementary Education through research, training, publication and extension. The National Policy on Education (1986 and 1992) provided for improving Teacher Education through upgrading service conditions, pay scales and curricula for various Teacher Training Institutes. The Main thrust of the NPE (1986) was to overhaul the Teacher Education which as elaborately discussed in the Programme of Action (1986 and 1992). The proposed action plan for the upgradation of Teacher Education programme was as follows:

(a) Launching of Centrally Sponsored Scheme of Teacher Education with financial assistance from the Centre to provide in-service training to all teachers at an interval of five years through District Institutes of Education and Training (DIETs). Institutes of Advanced Study in Education (IASEs), and Colleges of Teacher Education (CTEs).

(b) The induction and continuing training programmes for the Teacher Educators through NCERT and National Institute of Educational Planning and Administration (NIEPA).

(c) Launching of special orientation programmes for school teachers.

(d) Strengthening of SCERTs for making them independent and autonomous.

(e) Providing statutory status to NCTE to lay down norms, standards and guidelines for Teacher Education Courses, promoting co-ordination and linkages amongst various constituents of Teacher Education system, laying down norms, standards and guidelines for programmes of continuing education and professional development of Teachers and Teacher Educators and advising the Central Government, State Government, UGC, Universities and other agencies in all matters relating to Teacher Education and its development.

(f) Establishment and strengthening of Departments of Education in the Universities.

The revised NPE and POA (1992) emphasized: (i) greater accountability of teachers, (ii) provision of improved student services, (iii) better students behaviour norms, (iv) better facilities to Training Institutions, and (v) creation of a system of performance and appraisal of Training Institutions according to set standards.

The Report of the Review Committee (1990) reiterated the provisions envisaged in the Policy document which included: (i) the selection of students through stringent aptitude and attainment test for the programme, (ii) introduction of competence-based training programme, (iii) effective orientation to the programmes like development of attitude towards profession and society, (iv) organization of the need-based In-service and Refresher courses, and (v) strengthening the programme by supplying relevant learning materials, including journals, along with other needs to revamp the existing programme.

On the implementation of the NPE (1986) and the revised NPE (1992), the Centrally Sponsored scheme of Teacher Education was launched in the State.

The DIETs, IASEs and CTEs were established in Orissa. By 1995 there were 55 ST schools, 13 DIETs, 6 CTEs (Colleges of Teacher Education) and 3 IASEs (Institutes of Advanced Study in Education). In the meantime, the SIE was upgraded to SCERT and was given the status of Directorate of Teacher Education to conduct and supervise the training programmes and Teacher Education Institutes in the state. Now commercialization of Teacher Education has been stopped by an Act of Legislation in 1989 by abolishing all private Training Colleges and Training Schools. Teacher effectiveness has been given more importance with a view to improving students' performance and as such, Teacher Educators have been given a higher professional and academic status.

To sum up, training of teachers was viewed, almost without exception, as a pre-eminent pre-requisite to build up professionalism in the Teacher Education programme. Professionalism is acquired through exposure to credible Teacher Education courses; it is never ascribed. Teachers with capability, competence and commitment were considered prime-movers for quality education. Hence, unqualified emphasis was laid on Teacher Education at all times in pre-Independent as well as post-Independent India. More particularly, the Post-NPE India witnessed a substantially impressive expand development of the system of Teacher Education with uncompromising focus on quality and relevance.

3

Studies on Teacher Eduction

3.1 NEED AND IMPORTANCE OF REVIEW

Any investigation, whatever the scale involves reading what other people have written about the area of researcher's interest, gathering information to support or refute arguments and writing about findings.

Review of related literature is a preliminary task and an essential step in educational research. It enables the researcher to identify the studies and standard works that are related to his/her own research project. It develops an understanding of and insight into his/her research work and provides the necessary guidelines for going ahead on the right lines so that his/her project will be based on a rational footing and there would not be any unnecessary duplication and wastage of energy. Mouly (1964, p. 112) aptly remarks, "The review of the literature is an exciting task calling for a deep insight and clear perspective of the overall field. It is a crucial step which invariably minimises the risk of dead-ends, rejected topics, rejected studies, wasted efforts, trial and error activities already discarded by previous investigators and even more important erroneous findings based on a faulty research design. The review of literature promotes a greater understanding of the problem and its crucial aspects and ensures the avoidance of unnecessary duplication. It also provides comparative data on the basis of which it would be possible to evaluate and interpret the significance of one's findings. In addition, it contributes to the scholarship of the investigator."

The review of related literature is, therefore, an important aspect of research process. Most of the human knowledge can be found in books and libraries. For any worthwhile study in any field of knowledge, the researcher needs an adequate familiarity with the relevant literature. This research for reference material is a time consuming but fruitful phase of research programme. Every researcher must know what sources are available in his/her field of enquiry, which of them she/he is likely to use and where and how to find them. To quote Best (1982, pp. 40-41): "A summary of the writings of recognised authorities and of previous research provides evidence that the researcher is familiar with what is already known and what is still unknown and untested. Since effective research is based upon past knowledge, this step helps to eliminate the duplication of what has been done and provides useful hypothesis and helpful suggestions for significant investigation." In addition to giving ideas about approaches and methods to be appropriately used, review helps the researcher to devise a theoretical or analytical framework as a basis for the analysis and interpret of data.

Underscoring the need of review of related literature, Koul (1988, p. 83) has also stated, "Research takes advantage of the knowledge which has accumulated in the past as a result of constant human endeavour. It can never be undertaken in isolation of the work that has already been done on the problems, which are directly or indirectly related to a study proposed by a researcher. A careful review of the research journals, books, dissertations and other sources of information on the problem to be investigated is one of the important steps in the planning of any research study."

Thus, a review of the related literature must precede a well-planned research study. Complete survey of related literature gives the researcher necessary insight into the problem. It enables him/her to put forth vigorously the rationale for the study. It thus becomes an important part of the thesis as such to orient the readers with types of research that has been conducted in the field. Good, Barr and Scates (1941, pp. 104-05) analysed the purpose of review as:

(i) To show whether the evidence already available solves the problem adequately without further investigation.
(ii) To provide ideas, theories, explanations or hypotheses valuable in formulating the problem.
(iii) To suggest methods of research appropriate to the solution of the problems.
(iv) To locate comparative data useful in the interpretation of results.
(v) To contribute to general scholarship of the investigator.

Thus, review of related literature is of immense help to the researcher. One should be familiar with the locations and the use of the sources of educational information and without such a skill, he is lost simply as a hunter in the forest. In the words of Borg and Gall (1983, p. 142) "The literature in any field forms the foundations upon which all future work will be built."

This is how a brief analysis of the previous related studies in journals, magazines, reports and reference books is necessary and is of tremendous importance not only to formulate hypotheses but also to determine the tools and techniques to be employed for collection of data and to decide the method to be adopted for analysis and interpretation of data. In short, no viable research study can be carried out without a critical review of literature.

3.2 RELATED RESEARCH LITERATURE

The specific purpose of the review of related literature in the context of the present study is to identify, examine and summarise the comparable studies relating to the project entitled **"An Academic and Professional Profile of Teacher Educators at the Elementary Education Level."** Indian studies in which Teacher Educators of training institutes were taken as sample and closely related to the present research study have been reviewed.

Arora and Chopra (1969) offers an excellent study of status of Teacher Educators working in Elementary Teacher Training Institutions, Department of Teacher Education, NCERT, New Delhi. The purpose of the investigation was to study the socio-economic and educational background of Teacher Educators in Elementary Teacher Training Institutions of various states. Data were collected through a questionnaire about personal data, educational background, occupational background, information about work, economic status, family and social affiliations. The sample included 318 Teacher Educators. The responses were analysed in terms of percentage. Some of the salient findings are the minimum qualification of the Teacher Educators at elementary teacher training institutions were graduation or diploma in education; about 40% were better qualified, 2% had first division and 25% had secured second division at master's degree. Mostly, Teacher Educators had teaching experience in secondary schools which ranged from 5 to 30 years. The majority of teachers has to teach at least two subjects, 30% had to teach one subject, 40% two subjects, 19% three subjects and 4% four subjects. Some Teacher Educators had to do examination work and most of them had to do clerical work. No in-service education programme was organised for Teacher Educators. The majority of respondents were satisfied with their jobs and 62% of them did not want to change their profession. Dissatisfaction of the remaining teachers was mainly due to low income, low social prestige attached to the profession, no further prospects, unjust and unfair administration, heavy workload, political interference in admission and examination work.

Banarejee (1967) reported that 'The objectives of the study were to assess the needs of primary teachers' training from the viewpoint of qualitative and quantitative aspects and to suggest remedies, and to prenounce a few ideas that might uphold a training institution of tomorrow.

An interview schedule was prepared covering the different aspects of training of primary teachers viz. aims and objectives of training, organisation, curriculum and syllabus, practice-teaching, community living, examination, teaching staff, wastage, supervision, community development, in-service training and pay and allowances. Different educational authorities in sixteen states of India were interviewed with the help of this schedule. The findings of the study include: that the in-service education of primary teachers should be thought very important for enabling the teacher to grow intellectually in the course of his daily class-room work. The teacher should be kept up-to-date regarding new developments in the field of education. To remove the backlog of untrained teachers and to improve their academic and professional qualification, summer courses should be introduced.

Sharma (1970) investigated the Professional Needs of Teacher Educators of Undergraduate Training Institutions of Madhya Pradesh and Maharastra, Major objectives of the study were: (i) to establish the objectives of undergraduate teacher education (ii) to investigate into the present educational, professional and economic status of Teacher Educators in service, (iii) to study the procedure of recruitment and service conditions of Teacher Educators, (iv) to investigate into the professional needs of in-service Teacher Educators, and (v) to suggest measures for meeting the professional needs of in-service teacher educators in particular and pre-service Teacher Educators in general, in the light of the findings. The sample of the study consisted of 650 Teacher Educators, 130 principals and 100 experts from 130 primary training institutions of Madhya Pradesh and Maharastra. The research tools used were: (i) a rating scale for establishing the objectives of undergraduate teacher training, (ii) a questionnaire for Teacher Educators, (iii) a questionnaire for the principals, (iv) a rating scale for identifying the professional needs of Teacher Educators, and (v) an interview schedule.

The study revealed that objectives of undergraduate teacher education included development of personal qualities like open mindedness, self-discipline, tolerance, intellectual boldness, positive attitude towards children and profession and understanding of the problems and skills of handling them. Majority of the people who were interviewed expressed their dissatisfaction at the impact of teacher training on improving the teaching competence of teachers.

Professional needs of the Teacher Educators included: (i) a well-equipped library with latest literature in the field of education and research, (ii) facilities for attending meetings of professional organisations, (iii) developing skills in supervision of teaching and in the preparation of teaching aids, and (iv) provision for academic tours and study leave.

Arora, *et. al.* (1974) in their study, "The National Survey of Teacher Education at Elementary Level", reported that the project was undertaken with an objective of collecting data concerning major areas of Elementary Teacher Education such as students and staff, facilities and services, programmes, administration and supervision, etc. for: (i) compiling a National Report which could be used as a reference document, and (ii) locating weak areas which needed strengthening and drawing special attention of the NCERT. The major findings of the study were as follows: (i) about 59.7% of institutions were located in urban areas while 40.3% in the rural areas, 54.71% institutions were residential in nature, 22.84% were partly residential and the rest were not residential, 46.30% of the institutions were co-educational, 35.89% were for men only and 17.01% were for women only, 63.18% of institutions were run by State Government, 27.34% were run as private aided and 9.4% were as private unaided, (ii) quite a fair justice was done to the selection of candidates for admission to training institutions, the main criterion being the marks obtained at the Matriculation Examination, some seats were kept reserved for Scheduled Castes, Scheduled Tribes and deputed teachers too; there was a nice provision for stipend in almost all the Government Training Institutions in majority of the states, no tuition fee was charged, (iii) in majority of the states, the minimum qualification required for the recruitment to the post of principal as well as the teacher was a trained graduate, (iv) in most of the states, the syllabus was prescribed by the State Department of Education, most of the theory papers in different States were almost the same, (v) in many of the States, the trainees had to practice on major and one subsidiary craft, (vi) in most of the states, the final examination was conducted by the state Departments of Education usually, there was internal and external assessment for theory papers, practice teaching and crafts, (vii) poor physical facilities were observed in respect of science laboratories, inadequate buildings, inadequate accommodation in the hostels, no good libraries, no trained librarians and no adequate books and magazines, (viii) in case of Government institution, the grants from the Government formed the only source of income, in case of Private aided institutions also, considerable responsibility was borne by the Government and Private unaided institutions the main source of income was contribution from the management, donations, income from fees, etc. and (ix) some senior officers from the Directorate of Education inspected the institutions and provided academic as well as administrative guidance.

Dasgupta (1977) in an exploratory study into the factors affecting teacher efficiency and their implications for Teacher Training Program at the Primary Level, reported that the objectives of the study were: (i) to identify the characteristics, both personal and professional, that are considered as the constituents of teacher efficiency by various levels of educational personnel, (ii) to find out the situational factors that influence the teacher in performing his job to the best of his abilities, and (iii) to find out the implications of the findings for improving the teacher training program at the primary level. The study involved headmasters and teachers of primary schools. As a part of the study, a rating scale was developed and fifty primary schools were involved for the main study. Central tendency, Kendal's Co-efficient of Concordance Test and chi-square techniques were used for the analysis of data. The major findings of the study, are: (i) twenty-four personal characteristics of teachers had an influence on the growth and development of children, were identified, (ii) eleven professional competencies, which were linked with the attitude of teachers to self-learning were identified, (iii) the efficiency of the teacher was affected by the presence of certain factors, such as human relationships, socio-economic background of the teachers, organisation of training programmes, out of school activities assigned to the teacher and socio-cultural setting of the community, (iv) the personal characteristics of the teachers found insignificant.

Goyal (1980) in his project, "A Study of the Relationship among attitudes, job satisfaction, adjustment and professional interests of Teacher Educators in India", observed the following, taking the objectives as: (i) to measure attitudes, job-satisfaction, adjustment and professional interests of Teacher Educators of different categories based on sex, age qualification and experience, (ii) to find out the difference in attitude job satisfaction, adjustment and professional interests of Teacher Educators based on sex, age, qualification and experience, and (iii) to predict job satisfaction of Teacher Educators by treating their attitudes, adjustment and professional interests as independent variables.

The sample of his study consisted of 314 Teacher Educators working in thirty-eight institutions, which included men and women of different age groups possessing different qualifications and teaching experience. The major findings of the study were: (i) a large majority of the Teacher Educators were favourably inclined towards their profession and were satisfied in the job. However, they were not well adjusted and had low professional interest, (ii) the attitude and job satisfaction of different groups did not differ significantly, (iii) a majority of the Teacher Educators increased with age, (iv) professional interest among Teacher Educators increased with teaching experience in a school, (v) attitude, job satisfaction and occupational adjustment among Teacher Educators were associated with one another, whereas social and emotional adjustment and professional interest were not related with other variables, and (vi) job satisfaction could be predicated by attitude and occupational adjustment.

Hemambujam (1983) in his critical study of Teacher Education at the Secondary level in Tamil Nadu, reported that the main objectives of the study were: (i) to conduct a survey of teacher education of secondary level and make a critical appraisal of the B.Ed. program in Tamil Nadu, at its operational set-up, (ii) to report briefly on the historical background and the evolution of teacher education at the secondary level in India and especially in Tamil Nadu, (iii) to report a comparative study of the contemporary teacher education programs at the secondary level in advanced countries abroad with reference to that on India and in Tamil Nadu, and (iv) to locate the deficiencies in the system here, if any, and suggest remedies. The findings of the study were: (i) the State Government controlled the recruitment of all the Teacher Educators and the salaries were directly paid, (ii) the comprehensive B.Ed. curriculum was not effectively implemented due to time shortage, semester, internal assessment, etc. (iii) the revised B.Ed. syllabus lacked in content knowledge of the academic subjects, (iv) Teacher Educators follow the latest methods in teacher education programs due to the proper facilities prevalent in their colleges of education, (v) many colleges of education had hostels for the trainees and staffs and some had compulsory residential programs, and (vi) the financial resources of the colleges of education included tuition fees and special fees, remitted to them by the trainees and work experience was provided to the trainees through NSS Program.

Goyal and Chopra (1984) in their project "A Comparative Study of Teacher Profiles in the Rural and Urban settings in Elementary School System", mentioned that the major objectives of the project were: (i) to study and compare teacher profiles in respect of background, professional and socio-economic variables in elementary schools of rural and urban areas, educationally backward and advanced states, rural and urban areas of educationally backward states, and rural and urban areas of educationally advanced states, and to study and compare male and female teachers' profiles in respect of socio-economic status and psychological variables in elementary schools. The sample of study consisted of 450 teachers (233 from rural areas and 227 from urban) from 177 schools selected randomly for the study. The major findings of the study were: (i) more male teachers were working in rural areas and in backward states compared to urban areas and advanced states, (ii) a majority of teachers were found in the age-group of 30-40 years, having more than 11 years of experience, working in permanent capacity and were married, (iii) mostly teachers belonging to scheduled castes, tribes and backward classes were found in the schools of urban and backward states, (iv) teachers in urban areas and backward states were more qualified than their counterparts in rural areas and advanced state, (v) the work-load of the backward states teachers was comparatively heavier, (vi) teachers working in rural areas and in advanced states got more opportunities to attend in service programs than those in urban areas and in the backward states, (vii) no significant disparity was found between male and female teachers of rural and urban areas and educationally backward and advanced states in respect of socio-economic status and attitude towards the teaching profession, (viii) reading material was purchased by more urban teachers than rural teachers, (ix) more teachers of rural areas and in advanced states were members of professional organisations, but a large number of teachers in urban areas and in the backward states were members of social and cultural organisation, (x) job satisfaction among advanced state teachers found to be higher than that of backward state teachers, and (xi) rural and female teachers had less empathy, with understanding of their colleagues feelings and needs than urban and male teacher.

Saran (1975) in his study, "Teacher's Attitude towards Teaching Profession and certain Personality Variables as related to their Level of Education and Amount of Experience" reported that the hypotheses were: (i) attitude towards teaching profession is positively related with interest in literacy matters, level of adjustment, need of achievement, need of abasement, need of autonomy, need of endurance and level of education, (ii) positive relationship exists between level of education and adjustment, level of education and need of achievement, level of education and need of endurance, teaching experience and adjustment, teaching experience and need of autonomy and teaching experience and need of endurance. The findings were: (i) The attitude of teachers towards the teaching profession was positive. (ii) interest was positively related with attitude towards the teaching profession. The teachers who held a positive attitude showed more interest in literacy and mechanical fields. Teachers with negative attitude showed more interest in the field of agriculture and sports. (iii) Adjustment and attitudes were not directly related to each other. (iv) The needs of achievement, abasement, endurance and autonomy had hardly any influence on the formation of attitude towards teaching profession. (v) Level of education was positively related to degree of attitude towards the teaching profession. (vi) Level of education had no relationship with home adjustment. (vii) Teaching experience and adjustment were not significantly related. (viii) Needs of achievement and abasement were closely related to the level of education. (ix) The amount of experience and need of achievement were positively related to each other. (x) Need of abasement was positively related to the amount of experience. (xi) The needs of autonomy and endurance showed no relationship with amount of experience.

Seetharamu and Usha (1984) in their project "Pre-primary teacher Education—A Survey," pointed out that the objectives of the study were: (i) to survey the physical facilities available in institutions which trained teachers at pre-primary level, (ii) to draw profiles of trainees and teaching staffs in those institutions, (iii) to study the academic institutions, and (iv) to examine the financial status and problems of institutions. The major findings were: (i) a majority of the institutions were located in district/taluka headquarters. In urban areas most of the teachers at pre-primary level were women, (ii) all the teacher training institutions of the state were unaided and managed by private bodies, (iii) the medium of instruction in institutions was Kannada, which was the regional language. A few institutions had Urdu, Marathi and English as the medium of instruction, (iv) a majority of the institutions reported that they had adequate physical facilities such as class-rooms, amenities such as water, electricity, sanitation and space for out-door activities, (v) a majority of the institutions had trained teaching staff employed on a fulltime basis, (vi) academic programs in institutions comprised regular lecture classes and practice in teaching work, at regular intervals, (vii) a majority of the institutions provided a minimum of two demonstration lessons for trainees. Other than the prescribed programmes, institutions provided for physical education, craft work, drawing and music, besides first aid classes, citizenship camps, study visits and educational tours, (viii) facilities such as audio-visual aids and library facilities were available in most of the institutions, (ix) evaluation practices were carried out by institutions as prescribed by the State (Department of Education), (x) a detailed analysis of the financial status of the institutions revealed that their sources of income were fees collected from trainees and management contribution. The expenditure on equipment, library and institutional materials was meager. Teachers' salaries constituted the single largest expenditure.

Seetharamu and Manvikar (1986) in their study "Secondary Teacher Education—A Status Survey" said that it was a status study of institutions of teacher training at secondary level and the status of Teacher Educators working therein. The institutional status in terms of physical facilities, admission procedure and finance, individual status of Teacher Educators in terms of personal, social economic and professional status were investigated. Even through the universe of the study comprised 17 colleges and 158 Teacher Educators, responses could be obtained from only 11 institutions and 76 staff members working therein. The major findings were: (i) most of the institutions were located in Bangalore city and the majority of them were non-residential in nature, with a strength of 100 or less, (ii) most of the institutions were run independently except three which formed a part of chain of institutions run by a centralised management, (iii) most of the institutions had adequate facilities of demonstration-cum-practice teaching schools attached to them, (iv) library facilities were better in aided institutions as compared to those in unaided institutions, (v) the receipts and expenditure of aided institutions were much higher than those in unaided institutions. Some of the institutions collected capitation fee, (vi) the output of students from aided institutions was better than that of unaided institutions, (vii) the unaided institutions mostly attracted unmarried women, with a consolidated salary which was not so in aided institutions which had mostly married male members on the staff, (viii) the work-load for staff was greater in unaided institutions, (ix) most of the staff were post-graduate degree holders in education and having teaching experience in school level, (x) the workload for staff members ranged between three periods to eighteen periods per week. Supervision of lessons ranged between 200-500 lessons per year, (xi) the salary status of teachers ranged from Rs. 900 for teachers in aided institutions, Rs. 700/- in unaided institutions, (xii) facilities available for teachers in aided institutions were much better than those available for staff in unaided institutions, (xiii) most of the teachers belonged to Karnataka State and were Hindus, a majority of them were Brahmins, and (xiv) only a few staff members had attended state level seminars/conferences.

Srivastava (1986) in his study of "Qualities, Values, Attitudes, Activities and Adaptation of Teacher Educators" reported that the objectives of the investigation were: (i) to study the social, economic and educational qualities of Teacher Educators, (ii) to know the quality of their work, (iii) to study their service conditions, participation in curricular activities, etc., (iv) to study their job satisfaction and its relationship with their qualities, and (v) to give suggestions for improving conditions of Teacher Educators.

The investigation was a survey type study. The sample of the study consisted of 73 Teacher Educators working in all the then affiliated colleges of Avadh University having B.Ed. class. The main findings of the study were: (i) Teacher Educators were mostly upper caste Hindu, male, married and were permanent in service. None of the training departments of college had female Teacher Educators. (ii) The educational background of the Teacher Educators was of medium level. (iii) They were not found to be interested in curricular activities during their student life, a few Teacher Educators had also experience of teaching at primary level. (iv) The teacher colleges differed in size due to the different nature of the activities of the faculty. The professional activities of Teacher Educators were found to be affected due to large number of students. (v) Facilities of library, reading room, staff rooms, etc. were not up to the mark in the institutions. (vi) The socio-economic condition of Teacher Educators was generally satisfactory. Examinership was the only source of additional income for a majority of educators. (vii) The work-load of theory and practice teaching and other activities were not uniform in different institutions. However, in spite of various odds in working conditions, the educators seemed to be satisfied with their job.

Srivastava (1986) in her study of "Job Satisfaction and Professional Honesty of Primary School Teachers" reported that the objectives of the study were: (i) to examine the extent of job satisfaction and professional honesty among primary school teachers, and (ii) to make suggestions for creating a suitable environment in primary education in the above context. The sample of the study consisted of 100 educational experts, University/College teachers, administrative staff, etc. and 987 (363 female and 624 male) primary teachers. The findings of the study were: (i) the primary teachers of the area were found to have high job satisfaction and professional honesty, (ii) female teachers, as compared to male teachers, unmarried teachers as compared to married teachers, urban teachers as compared to rural teachers were significantly higher in job satisfaction and professional honesty, (iii) young teachers as compared to old teachers, junior teachers as compared to old teachers, and high academic achiever teachers as compared to low achiever teachers were also significantly higher in job satisfaction, (iv) caste was not found to have a significant effect on either of the two, (v) the major factors of job satisfaction among the primary teachers were inadequate salary, lack of physical facilities (space, equipment, etc.), problems in getting exploited by officers, etc., (vi) the major factors conducive to professional honesty in primary teachers were the teachers' strong and good character, the teachers' sincerity towards work, recognition and appreciation of the teachers' good work, a healthy and open environment in the school, the teachers' mental health, etc., and (vii) professional honesty were higher than job satisfaction.

It was reported in the **National Survey of Teacher Education at Elementary Level** (1977) that the elementary Teacher Educators had no special orientation for teaching in elementary teacher training institutions. Most of them did not have teaching experience in primary schools. With secondary school background, they did prepare teachers for the elementary level. The non-availability of science and craft teachers ETTIs was also reported in the survey.

While evaluating the usefulness of the orientation programme for the Teacher Educators, Srivastava (1982) reported that the dissatisfaction of college principals and Teacher Educators at the existing functioning of such programme. He also reported that the Teacher Educators were not very clear about the objectives of the programme. Singh and Malhotra (1987) recognised the need to train the Teacher Educators for training student-teachers. They recommended undertaking studies linking Teacher Educators, characteristics or classroom behaviour with student-teachers attainment in theory and teaching skills.

McCullough (1992) conducted a study to determine bio-demographic characteristics of Ohio prospective Teacher Educators and their motives for choosing the career of Teacher Educators, and the associations between the two. The term 'teacher-educator' refers to doctoral students enrolled in Ohio College of Education in specific programs who desire to teach pre-service teachers upon completion of Doctorate. The researcher discovered the changing profile of prospective Teacher Educators over the college for which it was proposed to revise recruitment and admission policies or re-evaluate doctoral programs preparing Teacher Educators to reflect this change. It was also found that the potential for professional productivity is released to some bio-demographic variables.

Reynolds (1992) while explaining the professional self-esteem of Teacher Educators reported that the Teacher Educators expressed positive belief about themselves and the value of their work, but they did entertain doubts about their acceptance and the acceptance of their discipline on campus. When questioned on the beliefs of their academic peers the negativity was almost universal. When gender provided very little, the type of institution was found contributing for the belief variations. Younger members of the faculty tended to be more pessimistic than older members of the faculty. Researchers took a more stringent approach to standards and rigour in teacher-education.

Davidman (1993) developed an assessment scheme to evaluate multi-cultural teacher education curricula. There search design probed student teachers knowledge, understanding, and abilities to implement the multicultural principles in their practice teaching assignments. It also probed the knowledge and understanding levels of the co-operating teaches and university faculty who supervised the candidates in their practice or student teaching assignments. The findings, in general, suggested that student teachers and the co-operating teachers and supervisors who were responsible for guiding candidates professional development, demonstrated only superficial levels of understanding related to multicultural education.

The Fifth Survey of Educational Research (1988-92), Vol. I have given trend reports in Teacher Education (1997, pp. 449-64). In this no more relevant studies are found to have been reported, but Joshi (*ibid.*, p. 451) has mentioned that a profile of female B.Ed. student-teachers in terms of self-image, value orientation, family size, academic achievement was developed by Gupta and Srinivasan (1990), and factors responsible for selecting teaching as a career as analysed by Sharma and Budhory (1991).

Mohanty (1998) conducted a study sponsored by NIEPA, New Delhi captioned "Profiles of outstanding Teachers and their contribution to the Development of Education." As many as 25 outstanding teachers of the state those who lived and worked over a century in different kinds of educational Institutions starting from primary to Sanskrit tols, including High Schools and ME Schools. This sample included Art and Science teachers working in tribal and coastal areas. Majority of them were trained, some of them were Headmasters and most of the teachers were good academicians with brilliant career. Majority of them were committed disciplinarian and had strong character, deep sense of honesty and integrity. They had sympathy and understanding for the students and the people among whom they worked. A few of them were very strong minded, determined and good social activists. All of them had organizing ability and were interested both in curricular and co-curricular activities. Some of them were eminent writers and few of them had histrionic ability. A few of them were quite saintly and well behaved having deep love for students and the profession. Most of them had great social concern and worked for social reform for removing old superstitions.

Some of them worked for Freedom struggle and sacrificed a lot for the national cause. Although there was no provision of State and National awards before independence, they were given highest honour of the community and reverence of the students, of course, after Independence, many of the outstanding teachers were given these awards. In conclusion, all these outstanding teachers immensely contributed to the development of education during that times.

Jena, *et. al.* (2001) in their study "Teacher Education in Orissa" jointly conducted by NCTE, New Delhi and Directorate of TE and SCERT, Orissa briefly reported the historical development and the present status as well as future perspectives of TE in Orissa. Since the study was under taken by the Directorate of TE itself, there is good amount of facts and figures or adequate quantitative data. It is heartening to note some of the free and frank views expressed in the report. These are as follows:

"In terms of background of DIETs faculty, 48 lecturers of 17 erstwhile defunct B.Ed Colleges representing 39.9% of TEs in position, 39 (32.0%) Secondary School Teachers selected by State Selection Board, 13 Secondary School Teachers (not selected), and 28 (18.0%) *adhoc* appointees are in faculty positions. Thus DIETs represent a mixed set of people. None of these groups except the Teacher Educators (TE) selected through the State Selection Board has been screened for their suitability in terms of qualification, experience, interest and other criteria" (pp. 73-74). "They (Secondary School Teachers) have found their way into DIETs for their own convenience, not for their suitability. That too quite a sizeable segment of this group does not have professional qualifications as envisaged in the DIET Guidelines or NCTE Norms and standards" (p. 74), "Principals are posted on *adhoc* basis on transfer. They are not screened for either aptitude or ability to head an academic institution like DIET. Therefore, the kind of vision and instructional leadership that is expected from principals is conspicuous by its absence" (p. 74).

Hence, the defective recruitment of faculty members in DIETs must have influenced adversely the quality of programmes implemented by them. By way of presenting facts about internal efficiency of DIETs, the report has stated the defective personnel policy and indifference towards DIET Guidelines for the lack of suitability of faculty members, particularly the needs of the DIETs. It has also lamented that "Largely, they, therefore, lack the competency, capability and commitment which jeopardize the multifarious professional activities of DIETs. Transfers are made as and when expediency calls for a transfer. Transfer policy should ensure stable tenure and rational placement" (p. 75). The report has also pointed out the adhocism in the programmes of the DIETs and lack of research and field experimentations as "one of the weakest components."

The report has mentioned the lack of interest and utilization of new pedagogy and "heavy hangover of the conventional methodology." It has mentioned the inadequate number of working days and duration of instructional hours in training institutions, and lack of proper supervision and ineffectiveness of practice teaching which is of crucial importance in TE (p. 86). It has reported about very high percentage of marks unduly scored by students and for that the report apprehended, "Another hidden factor that might have contributed to the phenomenon of extraordinary performance is the fact that secondary school teachers who do not have the slightest acquaintance with TE course, evaluate answer scripts." (p. 91). A "serious concern" has been expressed (p. 97) for not organizing adequate number of in-service programmes despite no dearth of funds. Since SOPT was found more lucrative for DIET faculty and stringent financial norms were there for In-service Training Programmes, there was relatively low coverage of teachers under such progammes and more in SOPT (p. 101).

The Chapter VI of the Report has included in resource support institutions like Directorate of TE and SCERT, SIET, ELTI, DPEP, RIE and UNICEF, Orissa, has omitted the teacher-training institutions for teachers in Physical Education, Hindi and Sanskrit and Art Education.

Another study entitled "Development of Teacher Education in Orissa: A comprehensive and critical study for meeting the challenges of the 21st century" was conducted by Mohanty (2000-02). This was a project report submitted to

UGC, New Delhi under Emeritus fellowship for which data were collected from different sources with the help of questionnaire, opinionnaire, interview schedule and observation schedule. It was a meaningful documentation of the historical development of Teacher Education (TE) in the state both Pre-British, British and Post-Independence period. The Investigator has critically analysed the existing programmes and practices of TE both at the Pre-service and In-service levels. The problems were identified and constraints were looked into and suggestions were shortcome from various Teacher Educators, Supervisors and Administrators for streamlining entire TE process with a view to emerging issues in the 21st century.

The major findings of the study were: (1) Reorganisation of TE system started in 1988 under the aegis of NPE 1986/1992 has not yet been streamlined and the Program of Action 1986/1992 for improvement of TE have not been implemented to a great extent. It was, therefore, urgently required for early step to be taken for creation of cardre, recruitment and posting as per NCTE Norms and Guidelines. (2) Huge wastage of time and resources was evident over the years due to lack of timely policy decision and political interference resulting in mismanagement and lack of control of the Directorate on the field personnel and own staff. Therefore, this kind of mismanagement and political interference should be reduced to the minimum. (3) In view of emerging societal needs and conditions, curricula at the various stages of TE need be revamped and reoriented as early as possible. (4) Since present curricular transaction suffers from stereo type, traditional and irrelevant procedure and practices, innovative, flexible and student-friendly practices be introduced in the curriculum. (5) Co-curricular activities according to available resources and local talents be scheduled and organised throughout the year.

The National Policy on Education (NPE-1986) and Programme of Action (1992) discussed the present scenario of teacher education in its various aspects and recommended suitable strategies for implementation. The various Centrally Sponsored Schemes in Teacher Education were launched for orienting teachers in the main priorities and directions envisaged in the NPE (1986). In the Program of Action (1992), particularly at the Elementary Stage, District Institutes of Education and Training (DIETs) were recommended for providing In-service training and improving Teacher Education. Recommendations were also made for strengthening the SCERT, NCTE and so on, for maintaining and upgrading the standards of Teacher Education. The National Advisory Committee on Learning without Burden (1992) set-up on 1992 under the chairmanship of Prof. Yash Pal suggested ways and means for reducing the load on students, while improving quality of learning, including capability for life long self-learning and skill development.

The Eighth Five Year Plan (1992-97) envisaged the schemes of DIET and ST schools and has provided for strengthening the infrastructure of Teacher Education Institution. There were 13 DIETs and 55 ST Schools in the State. The Regional office of NCTE was established at Bhubaneswar, Orissa for Eastern Zone of India during the year 1995-96 with the assistance of Government of India. A large number of teachers would be covered through in-service programmes. Both institutional and reputed professional organisations would be encouraged to conduct in-service and refresher courses for teachers. Open Universities at the National and State levels would supplement the efforts of the existing Training Institutions. The bulk of seats in Teacher Training Colleges would be reserved for rural women.

Ninth and Tenth Five Year Plan (1997-2007) During Nineth and Tenth Five Year Plan, emphasis was laid on In-service training of teachers working in Elementary School during 1997-98. As many as more than 1,10,000 teachers were trained by DIETs. Fifty percent seats were reserved for untrained teachers in ST schools.

During Ninth Plan, four new DIETs were proposed to be established in the district of Rayagada, Gajapati, Bargarh and Puri.

During Tenth Plan, it was proposed to set-up new DIETs in the district of Malkangiri, Nawarangpur, Nuapada, Sonepur, Boudh. The Government of Orissa had decided to impart training to more than 10,000 untrained Elementary School teachers of the State through Distance Education mode, without causing any dislocation to the activities of the school during the year 2002-03.

By reviewing the related literature, it was found that studies on Teacher Education in India were not many and comprehensive. The Indian researchers had not paid much attention to the field of Teacher Education at the Elementary stage. A few studies were conducted on professional needs, status of Teacher Educators, attitude, job satisfaction and professional interests of Teacher Educators. There was no profile study of Teacher Educators on a comprehensive scale at the state, regional and national levels. No attempt has been made so far to study the demographic, academic and professional aspects of the Teacher Educators of Elementary Training Institutes in India. With the above mentioned considerations in mind, the present project was undertaken to provide quantitative as well as qualitative knowledge on demographic, academic and professional characteristics of the Teacher Educators at the Elementary Education Level of Orissa and to present a comparative picture of the DIETs and ST Schools of Orissa. In addition, a situational analysis of Elementary Teacher Education Programme has been attempted here in the context of NCTE norms and standards as well as Government of India Guidelines (1989).

4

Teacher Educators: Research Design

4.1 RATIONALE OF THE STUDY

India is the second largest country in the world and its population is 1027015247 (Census 2001). Sixty percent of its population is under 24 years of age and about eighty percent live in rural areas. It has been estimated that forty eight percent of population live below the poverty line. Similarly, in Orissa the total population is 36706920 (Census 2001). Unrestrained population growth requires a continuous expansion of educational facilities just to maintain the existing level. The literacy rate in India is about 65.38 percent (Census 2001) and in Orissa it is 63.61 percent (Census 2001).

According to the survey report of the Directorate of TE and SCERT, Orissa, 2001, there were 53,614 number of elementary schools in Orissa. In May 1986, the Indian Parliament adopted a National Policy on Education (NPE) and in August 1986 approved a detailed Programme of Action (POA) for its implementation. The NPE (1986) states the goals of Universalisation of Elementary Education and of eradication of illiteracy. In May 1988, a National Literacy Mission (NLM) was formally launched to tackle the programmes of illiteracy in a time-bound manner. To achieve the above objectives, the following modes of inputs inter alia be required: (a) Suitable strategies for learning of the disadvantaged groups, so as to provide them equal educational opportunity, (b) appointment of dedicated and competent teachers and instructors, and (c) providing suitable academic and physical resource support to the teacher instructors which would comprise: (i) training, guidance and advice, (ii) development of locally relevant teaching learning materials, (iii) evaluation and field studies, action research and experimentation for tackling specific local programmes encountered in achieving goals. The National Council of Educational Research and Training (NCERT), the National Council of Teacher Education (NCTE) and the Education Department of Human Resources Development (MHRD) have proposed several structural as well as curricular modifications in the Elementary Teacher Education Programme to fulfil the roles expected from a primary school teacher according to NPE (1986)/POA (1992). In accordance with the provisions of the POA (1992) and as per the modifications proposed by the central authorities, several changes have been made and are being undertaken in the field of Elementary Education Programme in Orissa.

The structural changes, that is, the changes in institutional infrastructure have been brought about and DIETs (District Institutes of Education and Training) have been established as per the Guidelines of MHRD (1989) to "provide academic and resource support at the grass-root level for the success of various strategies and programmes being undertaken in the areas of Elementary and Adult Education" (p. 4). The Pre-Service Elementary Teacher Education programme in the state is being organised in the Secondary Training Schools (STS) and DIETs. Even if both types of Elementary Teacher Education programmes are under the administrative control of the State Government, DIETs have been given superior status with distinctly more resources and manpower support over the schools as given in Table 4.2.

The present scenario, as evident from the Table 4.2 indicates duality in the institutional structure, which is being allowed to exist without any empirical basis. Research in

TABLE 4.1

DIET-wise Distribution of Primary and Middle Schools in the State

Sl. No.	Name of the DIETs	Name of district	No. of Block	No. of Primary schools	No. of M.E. Schools	Total	Total No. of Schools under each EIET
1	2	3	4	5	6	7	8
1.	Dhenkanal	Angual	08	1235	123	1558	3050
		Dhenkanal	08	1115	377	1492	
2.	Remuna	Balasore	12	1815	917	2732	4493
		Bhadrak	07	1239	522	1761	
3.	Sambalpur	Baragarh	12	1429	404	1833	
		Sambalpur	09	1006	238	1244	4385
		Deogharh	03	421	113	534	
		Jharsuguda	05	611	165	776	
4.	Tikabali	Boudh	03	591	111	702	2465
		Kandhamal	12	1519	244	1763	
5.	Balangir	Balangir	14	1933	389	2322	3259
		Sonepur	06	761	176	937	
6.	Khallikote	Ganjam	22	2936	695	3631	4676
		Gajapati	07	937	108	1045	

(Contd.)

TABLE 4.1 *(Contd.)*

1	2	3	4	5	6	7	8
7.	Dolipur	Cuttack	14	2177	667	2844	
		Jajpur	10	1516	678	2194	8651
		Jagatsinghpur	08	1179	421	1600	
		Kendrapara	09	1430	583	2013	
8.	Bhawanipatna	Kalahandi	13	1705	365	2070	2967
		Nuapada	05	731	166	897	
9.	Keonjhar	Keonjhar	13	1807	631	2438	2438
10.	Baripada	Mayurbhanja	26	2941	795	3736	3736
11.	Jaypore	Nawarangpur	10	1249	206	1455	
		Koraput	14	1853	236	2089	6213
		Malkangiri	07	898	103	1001	
		Rayagada	11	1482	186	1668	
12.	Khurda	Puri	11	1432	479	1911	
		Khurda	10	1262	415	1677	4688
		Nayagarh	08	826	274	1100	
13.	Sundargarh	Sundargarh	17	2068	523	2591	2591
	Total		314	42104	11519	53614	53614

Source: Directorate of TE & SCERT, 2001.

TABLE 4.2

Comparative Study Resource and Manpower Allocations for Elementary Teacher Education Programme of Orissa

Type of institution	*Unit Cost (in Rs.)*		*No. of Teaching Personnel*			*Non-Teaching Personnel*			
	1991-92	*1992-93*	*With P.G. degree*	*Trained graduate*	*Other types of teacher*	*Minis-terial staff*	*No. of miniial staff*	*Intake cap.*	*Min. ent. Qua.*
DIETs	10,430	11,430	22	02	06	09	06	50	+2
STSs	8,870	8,900	00	04	03	01	06	50	+2

Sources: Directorate of Teacher Education & SCERT, Orissa, Bhubaneswar.

TABLE 4.3

Circlewise distribution of STS, and DIETs in the State of Orissa

Sl. No.	Name of the Circle	No. of STSs	No. of DIETs
1.	Cuttack	6	Nil
2.	Jajpur	Nil	1
3.	Kendrapara	2	Nil
4.	Jagatsinghpur	1	Nil
5.	Balasore	3	1
6.	Bhadrak	3	Nil
7.	Khurdha	4	1
8.	Puri	4	Nil
9.	Dhenkanal	2	1
10.	Keonjhar	2	1
11.	Mayurbhanja	3	1
12.	Sambalpur	2	1
13.	Bolangir	3	1
14.	Kalahandi	2	1
15.	Phulbani	2	1
16.	Sundargarh	3	1
17.	Ganjam	5	1
18.	Koraput	2	Nil
19.	Jeypore	3	1
	Total	52	13

evaluating the relative efficacy of these two types of institutions was felt essential both at the national and state level. The justification for having two types of programmes was necessitated for close scrutiny when there was no differential utility of their outputs and the same curriculum was to be transacted in both types of Institutions.

When the ST schools followed the traditional methods and strategies of teaching and learning, the transactional philosophy of DIET was (i) to give training (both at induction level as well as continuing varieties), and (ii) to give resource support for Extension/Guidance activities and development of Teaching Learning Materials (TLM), Evaluation tools, etc. and for conducting Action Research.

FIGURE 4.1

Map of Orissa Showing the Location of DIETs and ST Schools under Study

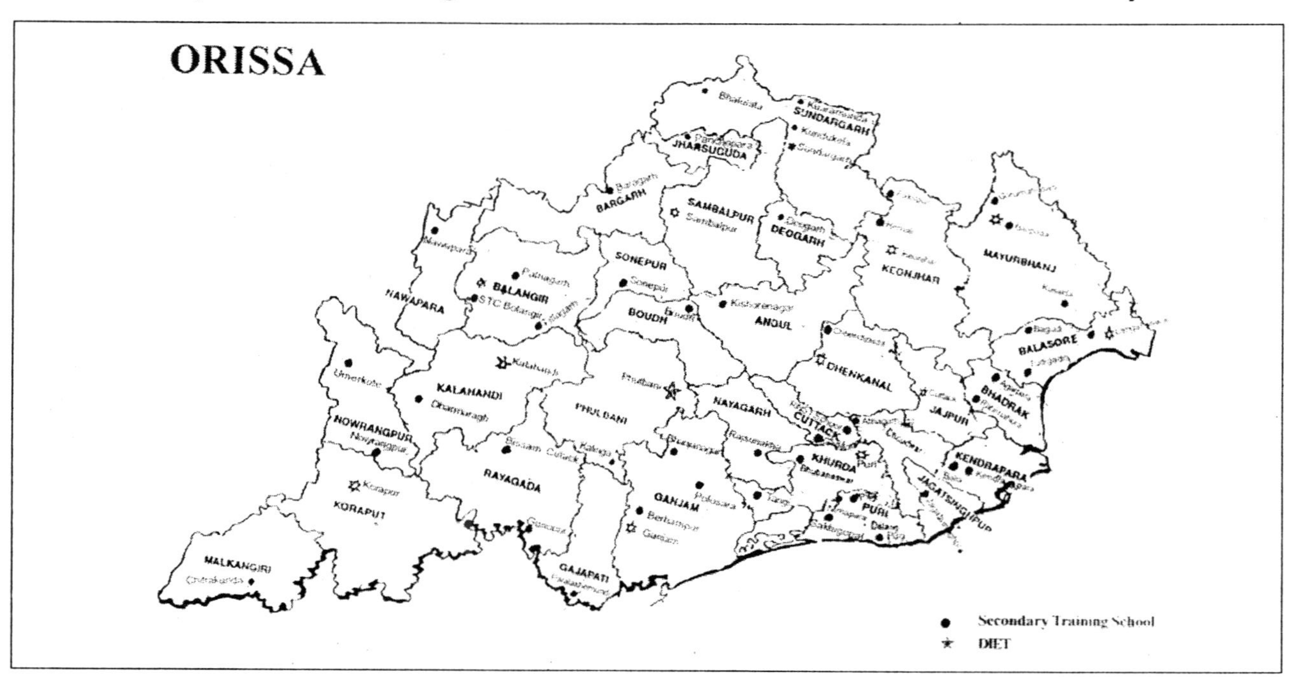

It may be seen from the Table 4.3 that there were 13 DIETs and 52 ST schools in Orissa. As per the approved staffing pattern, there were 544 Teacher Educators in both the institutions. With a view to the comparative status of the Teacher Educators' academic and professional growth and the difference in student teachers performance, the Investigator proposed to conduct the study entitle, **"An Academic and Professional Profile of Teacher Educators at the Elementary Education Level"** so that suitable action plan can be developed for improving the existing condition.

4.2 OBJECTIVES OF THE STUDY

(i) To collect demographic data of Teacher Educators of Orissa.
(ii) To know their academic background.
(iii) To ascertain their professional growth.
(iv) To compare the role preference *versus* role performance of Teacher Educators working in ST Schools and DIETs.
(v) To develop professional and academic profiles of Teacher Educators for initiating plan of action for improvement of academic and professional growth of Teacher Educators working in ST schools and DIETs.

4.3 DELIMITATION

The study was subjected to the following limitations:

1. It was confined to the Teacher Educators of DIETs and ST Schools.
2. The geographical area of the study was confined to the state of Orissa.
3. It was restricted to the full time Teacher Educators, Sr. Teacher Educators, Vice-Principals and Principals/Headmasters.
4. Further it was confined to three major aspects of the teachers profile, i.e. (i) demographic variables, (ii) academic variables, and (iii) professional

variables. All these variables were kept in focus of the study because they constitute the Teacher Educators academic and professional profile.

5. There were important dimensions like social commitment of the Teacher Educators, their psychological and political dimensions, which were deliberately excluded from the present study.

4.4 OPERATIONAL DEFINITIONS

The different terms involved in the present study have been defined as follows:

Academic

According to Chambers Dictionary (1988) 'academic' means a Platonic Philosopher one studying or teaching at a university, especially, one who has scholarly tastes.

According to Oxford Dictionary (1991) 'academic' means a member of scholarly institution.

According to the Encyclopaedia of America (1829) the title 'academic' conferred by a college or university, signifying that a certain step or grade has been attained in an area of learning. The term "academic" also means the award of a diploma conferring the bachelor's degree marking completion of an under-graduate study, the master's and doctor's degree reward for graduate study. In the study, it simply means the educational and cognitive variables.

Professional

Good (1973) in the Dictionary of Education defines 'professional' as one who has acquired a learning skill and conforms to ethical standards of the professional in which he practices the skill, 'professional school' means a higher education institution preparing students directly for the practice of a profession, traditional professional schools are those of law, medicine and theology which together with dentistry prepare students who have completed baccalaureate programmes, others include agriculture, business, engineering, home economics, library science, nursing and social services, all of which typically offer under-graduate professional study as well as under-graduate studies.

Goyal (1985) in his book, "The Indian Teacher Educator" defines professional as one of the academic achievement by way of obtaining additional degrees or diplomas, writing book, articles and papers, conducting research and membership of professional bodies and committees were considered to show interest of Teacher Educators in their profession.

According to Encyclopedia of America (1829), professional education is that form of education, which prepares students for professional callings or employment. It may be differentiated on the one hand from vocational education, which is prepared for employment in occupations not generally recognised as professions and on the other hand from general and liberal education which has no specific vocational application. However, as liberal education is organised in colleges and universities, it usually includes some specialisation in particular fields of study, aiming partly at assisting the graduate to earn a living. Thus, many colleges of liberal arts and sciences adopt their programmes to provide education in such fields as business administration, home economics and teaching.

In describing professional education, however, it is customary to include in the category only those form specialised higher education that are organised on separate schools, either as major units of universities or as independent institutions. On this basis there are some 20 fields of professional education in the United States, including agriculture, business, administration and engineering. The number of fields increases as new services, professional in character, are devised and developed and as extended courses of training leading to academic degrees are required for proficiency in rendering these services.

In the present study, Certified Teacher, B.Ed. and M.Ed. degrees are included under professional courses.

Profile

In the new Dictionary of Psychology, Harriman (1947) defines profile as an arrangement of test scores which indicates the relative standing of an individual on various psychological measures, e.g. linguistic, intelligence, educational achievement, status, etc. Good (1959), in the Dictionary of Education, defines it as any graphic technique usually a line diagram, that indicates the relative position of one person or a group on each of several tests of other measures. Agarwal and Biswas (1971) in the Encyclopedic Dictionary and Directory of Education, define the profile DL graph as a graph indicating the performance of an individual on a series of tests or a series of ratings of his personality traits. In the Dictionary of Behavioral Science, Wolman (1973) considers profile analysis as a procedure used in assessing an individual's uniqueness and trait organisation which consists of establishing pattern of traits in the profile of the individual.

Kerlinger (1981) defines 'profile' as a set of different measures of an individual or group, each of which is expressed in the same unit of measure. An individual's scores on a set of different tests constitute a profile, if all scores have been converted to a common measure system, like percentiles ranks and standard scores.

The common characteristics found in different definitions of the "profile" refer to the relative standing or position of a person or a group of persons on different aspects. Viewed in the context of the Teacher Educator, the word 'profile' implies the assessment and presentation of their demographic background, academic, professional, sociological and psychological characteristics. For the purpose of the present study, 'profile' refers to the demographic, academic and professional characteristics of Teacher Educators.

(a) **Demographic profile:** The term 'demographic profile' has been used to know the age, sex, religion, caste, place of birth, health, marital status and socio-economic status.

(b) **Academic profile:** The term 'academic profile' refers to academic career, teaching career, research activities, publication, participation in academic activities and awards received for academic achievements.

(c) **Professional profile:** The term 'professional

profile' refers to various professional aspects viz. discipline, rank, experience, professional background, participation in extension activities, attitude towards internal organisational variables, participation in different educational organisation and professional activities in foreign countries.

According to NCTE (1998, p. 23) teacher profile has been emanated from the context and concern that call for additional rates besides the conventional ones. The following capabilities and competencies need to be highlighted: Including the intrinsic and extrinsic values of professional competency. Professional commitment and professional ethics.

- Creating and reconstructing knowledge.
- Selecting, organising and using learning resources.
- Effectively transacting curriculum, selecting and organising educational activities and programmes for learners with special needs.
- Using media and appropriate instructional technologies.
- Communicating effectively and responding to the challenges of continuity and change.
- Counseling students for personality development, adjustment and learning attainment.
- Conducting research, especially action research and initiating innovative practices.
- Organising student activities.
- Inculcating a sense of value judgment, value commitment and value transmission.
- Understanding the importance of inter-relationship between culture and education and culture and personality.
- Fostering interest in lifelong learning.
- Understanding the aspiration and expectations of the community and establishing mutually supportive linkage between the school and the community.
- Acting as a change agent for modernisation and development.

The educational programme for prospective teachers, therefore, needs to be so designed as to develop in them the requisite skills, capabilities, and competencies.

Elementary Education Level

Elementary education is the period of formal schooling extending from admission to school in kindergarten or 1st grade to completion of the 6th, 7th and 8th grade. It also known as Primary education in many countries. It designates the range of schooling for children from about 6 to 12, 13 or 14 years of age.

Most countries of the world have adopted the principle that all citizens need at least an Elementary Education. Compulsory attendance laws have been enacted in the hope of assuring that children get at least 6 to 8 years of schooling. In practice, the proportion of children going to Primary schools ranges from nearly 100% in the more affluent nations to 60% or less in some of the developing nations. In many countries, Elementary schooling is the only formal education most people receive. In others, it considered the first step on a ladder that ideally leads to Secondary School and College. One basic task of Elementary schools around the world is to teach the "three R's." Reading, writing and arithmetic. Frequently, the schools try to inculcate attitudes and standards of value, many Elementary curricula go beyond the basics and introduce Science, Foreign language and Social studies. Methods of teaching range from formal instruction in the three R's to "Open Class Room" techniques that encourage each child to develop its own interests and learn at its own pace.

There are many groupings of the Elementary grades. In the United States grades 1 to 3 are often classified as primary, grades 4 to 6 a intermediate and grades 7 and 8 as upper. Some schools group grades 7 and 8 with grade 9 in Junior High Schools and consider this part of Secondary School. Other schools make 6, 7 and 8 Middle or Intermediate school, an Institution between Elementary and High School. In the present context, Elementary Education refers to education provided in grades I to VIII.

Primary Education

Primary Education generally denotes the basic or introductory schooling the young children receive, usually starting at 6 years of age and continuing to 10 to 12. The ages of starting and stopping vary.

In some school system, the Primary classes continues up to 5th grade, after which children who are continuing their education go on to Middle School. In other systems, the break between the Elementary and Secondary Schools comes after the 7th or 8th grade.

Primary education can be called the most universal and significant level of formal education in that far more of the world's people get schooling at this level than at the Secondary and Higher levels. UNESCO reports state that in Latin America about 91% of school age children are enrolled at the first or Elementary level, about 22% at the second level and about 3.4% at the third level. In Asia, about 53% are enrolled at the first level, 15% at the second and 0.4% at the third. In Africa, the corresponding figures are 51%, 9% and 0.4%. Highly developed countries such as the United States and Britain have virtually 100% of their younger children and 80% to 90% of Secondary School age children in schools.

The purposes of Primary education are influenced the proportion of children a country is educating at higher level. Where Primary schooling is the first and last formal education, the paramount aim is to teach basic skills to the children as reading, writing and simple arithmetic, Raising the literacy rate may be a major endeavour. The schools may also give time to such areas as history, citizenship and health. In the developed nations where a large share of children go to Secondary schools, the Primary schools still teach fundamental skills. They are also concerned, however, with preparing students to continue the educational ladder to High School and College. They may, for example, introduce the study of sciences and foreign languages for the children. The schools can also afford to give time to areas such as art and music with the aim of enriching the child's background. In case of the present study, Primary Education and Elementary Education are equivalent.

4.5 METHOD

The present study adopted the Descriptive-cum-Survey method and followed the allied strategies for its various aspects. A Descriptive Study describes and interprets what is or what exists. It is concerned with the conditions or relationships that exist, opinions that are held, processes that are going on, effects that are evident, or trends that are developing. It is primarily concerned with the present, although it often considers past events and influences as they relate to current conditions (Best and Kahn, 1986).

Various writers have classified Descriptive Studies differently. These classifications mostly range from the survey, which describes the status quo of educational variables to the co-relational study, which investigates the relationships between variables (Koul, 1980)

Survey research has contributed much to the methodology of the social sciences. Its most important contributions perhaps, have been to rigorous sampling procedures, the overall design and the implementation of the design of studies, the unambiguous definition and specification of research problems and the analysis of data. Survey researchers use a "flow plan" or chart to outline the design and subsequent implementation of a survey. The flow plan starts with the objectives of the survey, lists each step to be taken and ends with the final report. First, the general and specific problems that are to be solved are as carefully and as completely stated as possible.

Some survey researchers even design tables for the analysis of data at this point in order to clarify the research problems and to guide the construction of interview questions. The next step in the flow plan is the sample and the sampling plan. Once the universe is defined, a decision is made as to how the sample is to be drawn. Random samples are used in various survey research works, the next step is the construction of the interview schedule and other measuring instruments to be used. After drafts of the interview schedule and other instruments are completed, they are pre-tested on a small representative sample of the universe. They are then revised and put in final form. The steps outlines above constitute the first large part of any survey. Data collection is the second large part. The third large part of the flow plan is analytical. .The responses to questions are coded and tabulated. Tabulation is simply the recording of the number of types of response in the appropriate categories, after which statistical analysis follows: percentage, average, relational indices and appropriate test of significance. The analysis of the data are studied, collated, assimilated and interpreted. Finally, the results of this interpretative process are reported (Kerlinger, 1981).

Runkel and McGrath (1972) gave a typical project in terms of a survey research cycle. Thinking about survey research the need to consider a given survey project as an entity. Each stage has its implications for later stages. The diagram is given in Fig. 4.2.

In the descriptive survey method, no hypothesis need be used (Chandra and Saha, 1987). The survey method gathers data from a relatively large number of cases at a particular times. Survey means where the present conditions are described in some depth or detail, using any number of respondents. The teachers can be described by finding out their age, sex, interests, attitudes and other facts. A survey can be conducted with a segment of the population. Kerlinger (1981) has stated that survey information is accurate within sampling errors, or course. The accuracy of properly drawn samples is frequently surprising, even to experts in the field. A sample of 600 to 700 individuals or families can give a remarkable accurate portrait of a community—its values, attitudes and beliefs.

In 1969, the Carnegie Commission of Higher Education sponsored a series of large scale, parallel national surveys of the American under-graduate and graduate students, faculty and administrator. The faculty study, on which they drew most heavily, employed a questionnaire that was mailed to approximately 100,000 full time college and university professors located at 303 schools around country (Ladd and Lipset, 1975).

FIG. 4.2

Survey Research Cycle

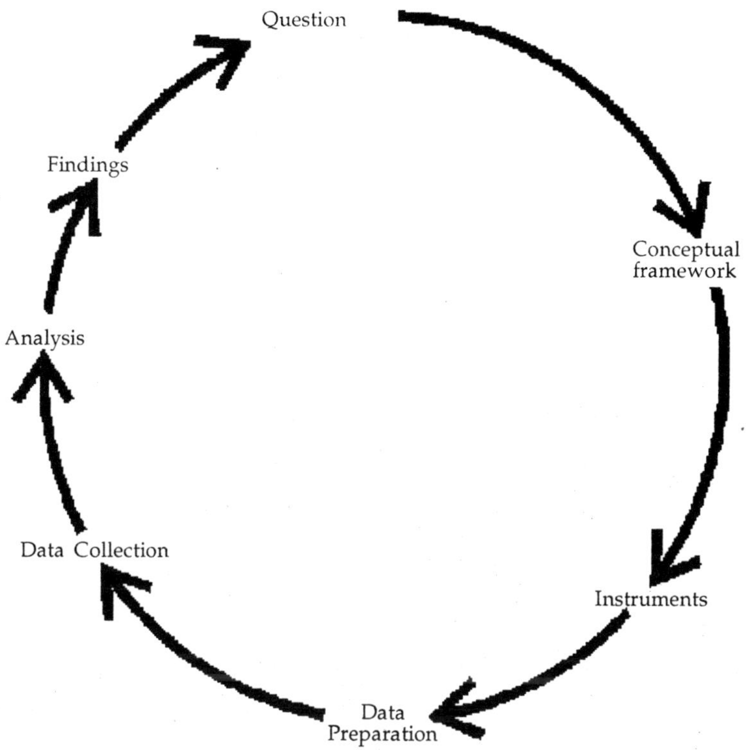

4.6 SAMPLE

A population refers to any collection of specified group of human beings or of non-human entities such as objects, educational institutions, geographical areas, time units, prices of wheat or salaries drawn by individually, etc. Some statisticians call it universe. A population containing a finite number of individuals, members or units is called a finite population. A population with infinite number of members is known as infinite population (Koul, 1980).

The population for this research study was finite population and consisted of all full-time Teacher Educators who were appointed by Government and were working in

TABLE 4.4

Distribution of Sample of the Primary Teacher Education Institutions

Sl. No.	Instruments	Type of Instituions	Total No. of Insti-tutions	No. of Insti-tutions, Individuals visited tools administered	No. of Responses (in %)
1.	Questionnaire	(i) STSs	55	Asst Teachers-106	241 (54.4)
		(ii) DIETs	13	TE-135	
2.	Opinionnaire	(i) STSs	55	HMs-14	14 (46.6)
		(ii) DIETs	13	Principal-11	11 (36.6)
				Experts in Edn.-5	5 (16.6)
3.	Observation Schedule	(i) Secondary Training Schools (STSs)	55	24 STS-24	24 (44.4)
		(ii) District Institutes of Education and Training (DIETs)	13	11 DIETs-11	11 (84.6)
4.	Interview Schedule	(i) STSs	55	Asst. Teachers-24	24 (44.1)
		(ii) DIETs	13	Teacher Educators-30	30 (54.4)

the State of Orissa. A sample is a small proportion of a population selected for analysis and interpretation. By studying the sample, certain inferences may be made about the population. Sampling tools save time, money and energy provide no means of probing into problems that are too widely to be tackled by conventional methods. No researcher can afford to be in familiar with sampling procedure and pitfalls that may be encountered when utilising them (Vandalen, 1965).

A sample so selected is called the random sample, in which each subject had an equal chance of selection. A modified form of random sampling and stratified sampling is a device, which ensures representativeness in selecting a sample for a population composed of subgroups or strata of different sizes.

In the present study, however, sampling was not done. The number of Teacher Educators in Orissa was about 554 in the year 1998. In order to give weightage to proportional allocation according to the strength of Teacher Educators in different DIETs and S.T. Schools and also to obtain adequate responses, it was decided to cover the entire population. The responses thus received would be taken as the representative sample. Table 4.3 presents the distribution of samples regarding Primary Teacher Education Institutions taken for the project.

4.7 RESEARCH TOOLS

(i) Questionnaire

"Teacher Educator Data Form" was developed and used for collecting data about demographic, academic and professional qualification of Teacher Educators.

(ii) An Opinionnaire

An Opinionnaire was developed and used for eliciting the opinions of experts on Teacher Education programme.

(iii) An Observation Schedule

An Observation Schedule was prepared and used for documentation of relevant information from records and documents of Elementary Teacher Education Institutions and also for getting the feedback and perception about the programme and policies being implemented and to be implemented in future.

(iv) An Interview Schedule

An Interview Schedule was developed and utilized for studying the relevance and adequacy of In-service Training Programmes conducted by the Teacher Educators.

4.7.1 Selection of Research Tool

The questionnaire was considered to be the most suitable tool for the present study. According to Drever (1965), 'Questionnaire is a series of questions dealing with some psychological, social, educational topics given to a group of individuals with regard to some problems, sometimes employed for diagnostic purpose, or for assessing personality traits.

Barr, Davis and Johnson (1935) have defined questionnaire as a systematic compilation of questions that are submitted to sampling of population from which information is desired. A questionnaire has the advantage of applying certain restrictions upon a situation: (i) it asks specific questions which call for specific answers, (ii) these answers can be classified, and (iii) the information contained in the responses can sometimes be quantified.

Questionnaires are of three kinds: (i) restricted or close-form, (ii) unrestricted or open-form, and (iii) pictorial form. For the present study the closed-form questionnaire was selected.

4.7.2 Construction of the Questionnaire

The review of the following research tools facilitated the construction of the questionnaire. The selection and adoption of items of the questionnaire for the present study was finalised with suitable modification that were found necessary and relevant for the Teacher Educators of Orissa.

(i) The teacher questionnaire Merelman: political Socialization and Educational Climates. Rinehart and Winstom, New York, 1971.
(ii) The Carnegie Commission Faculty study Questionnaire Ladd and Lipset: The Divided Academy McGraw Hill, New York, 1975.
(iii) General Faculty Survey Questionnaire, Basu, 1977.
(iv) Polytechnic Teacher Data Form Panjwani: Profile in Polytechnic Teachers in India, TTTI, Calcutta, 1982.
(v) University Teacher Data Form: Maiti, University of Calcutta, 1993.

TEACHER EDUCATOR DATA FORM (CONTENT STRUCTURE OF THE QUESTIONNAIRE)

Variables/Items Used in the Present Research Tool

1. Name and address
2. Age
3. Sex
4. Religion
5. Caste
6. Place of Birth
7. Mother Tongue
8. Health
9. Marital Status
10. Number of Children
11. Level of Education
12. Academic Qualification
13. Year and class in general and professional degree
14. No. of students enrolled
15. Interest lie primarily in teaching or in research
16. No. of books or monographs published
17. Presentation of papers in Seminars or Conference in State and National levels
18. In-service Education
19. Hobby
20. Department
21. Present Rank
22. Experience
23. Time spent per week in teaching and research, training and administration.
24. Attitude towards salary
25. Relation between teaching and nonteaching.
26. Research facility
27. Availability of fund
28. Relation with students
29. Committee member of any faculty or association
30. Foreign tour for any academic purpose
31. Research studies Conducted/Published

VALIDITY AND RELIABILITY OF THE RESEARCH TOOL

Validity and reliability are essential for any data-gathering instrument for its effectiveness.

Validity

According to Anastasi (1966), the validity of a test concerns what the test measures and how well it does so. In the words of Cronback (1949), 'A test is valid, to the degree that we know what it measures or predicts'. In other words, a test is valid in proportion as it measures well what it desires to be measured. The most important techniques to measure the validity of the test are as follows:

(i) Content Validity,
(ii) Predictive Validity,
(iii) Concurrent Validity, and
(iv) Construct Validity.

To determine the validity of the questionnaire, it was sent to five experts and they were requested to give their opinion on a five-point scale as excellent highly satisfactory, satisfactory, not satisfactory and poor. Ratings were obtained from them as excellent and highly satisfactory. Therefore, expert opinion was highly favourable in regard to the validity of the tool.

Reliability

According to Anastasi (1966), 'Reliability refers to the consistency of scores obtained by the same individual when re-examined with the same test on different occasions or with different sets of equivalent items. There are four methods of measuring the reliability of a test: (i) Test-retest method, (ii) Split-half method, (iii) Alternate or parallel form method, and (iv) Rational equivalence method. The item reliability was found out by using test-retest method and it was found that all the items are highly reliable.

Try-out

The questionnaire under the title **"Teacher Educator**

Data Form", containing 36 items was developed to fulfil the objectives of the study. To ensure the validity of the study, 10 eminent professors, covering all the education departments were requested to analyse the items of the questionnaire critically and to give their comments/suggestions for improvement. On the basis of the suggestions of the experts, the questionnaire was revised.

Then the **"Teacher Educator Data Form"** was administered personally on 40 known Teacher Educators including principals, vice-principals, and senior Teacher Educators of DIETs. After the tryout. the questionnaire was finalised, containing 25 items. The copy of the final form of the questionnaire (Teacher Educator Data Form) is attached in **Appendix A.**

The items like, caste, place of birth, health, class and rank in Bachelor Degree and Master Degree. Presentation of papers in seminars or conference at the national and international levels, attitude towards participation in extension activities, relationship between teaching and non-teaching staff, membership and fellowship of academic learning societies were included in consultation with the supervisor and on the suggestions of the experts.

The questionnaire was thus developed and finalised under the title **"Teacher Educator Data Form"** with the help of the different experts in Education and the Supervisor.

4.7.3 Opinionnaire

With a view to ensuring validity and reliability of data collected with the help of **"Teacher Educator Data Form"**, it was found necessary to develop an opinionnaire for eliciting the opinion of experts in the field of Education, particularly in Teacher Education. An opinionnaire is defined as a special form of enquiry used by the researcher for seeking the opinion of the related population sample on certain facets and factors of the problem under investigation. It enabled the investigator to collect the views on different facts of the problem under study, so that they can quantify the same, analyse, interpret and infer. According to Best (1981, p.192), an opinionnaire could be used "to measure opinions in many controversial areas, national integration merit rating of the teachers, universal military training and many others."

Hence, the opinionnaire has the following characteristics:

(i) It makes use of statement of questions on different aspects of the problem under investigation.
(ii) It solicited responses either a three point scale or five point scale.

The investigator, therefore, decided to elicit the views of the experts and veteran educationists on different aspects and factors of Teacher Education.

Taking into consideration the major components of an educational system, the Investigator developed a structured Opinionnaire to take the opinion of the experts in Education, regarding the status, present position and problems of Elementary Teacher Education Institutions. They are also requested to give advice for the qualitative improvement of Teacher Education in the state.

The Opinionnaire was individually administered by the Investigator on the personnel associated with the Elementary Teacher Education Programme at different levels. The schedule contains items on: (i) Present status of DIETs and ST schools, (ii) requirement of professional degree for Teacher Educators, (iii) minimum entry qualification required for the pupil-teachers for Elementary Teacher, (iv) how to increase interest of Teacher Educators to participate in co-curricular activities, (v) how to motivate them to contribute papers/ articles in their professional subjects, (vi) about the academic, administrative and financial problems, (vii) about the design duration and contents of Elementary Teacher Education, (viii) development of evaluation system, and (ix) suggestions about the improvement of Teacher Education at the Elementary Level. The Opinionnaire was prepared in consultation with a group of experts in Education.

4.7.4 Observation Schedule

This tool was meant for documentation of data and collection of feedback from the Teacher Education Institutions (DIETs and ST schools). The Investigator has sought to collect data from DIETs and ST Schools through her on-the-spot visits. It has been made as brief as possible to note her remarks in shortest possible time. The data were mainly relating to courses provided, total strength of staff members, student strength, examination results, duration of courses, problems faced in various areas starting from selection, admission of students to their examination and evaluation. Suggestions were also invited from the Heads of the Institutions and other staff members as "the wearer knows where the shoe pinches." Besides, there were scope for getting the perception of Teacher Educators/Pupil Teachers about Teacher Education for the coming decades. Data about innovations/good practices were also planned to be collected from the DIETs and ST schools. As far as possible, relevant and supporting reports/materials were also collected from the Institutions.

4.7.5 Interview Schedule

It was prepared as precisely as possible and there were ten items mainly under two heads: (i) Brief bio-data, (ii) Organisation of courses. This Interview Schedule was mainly intended for studying the relevance and adequacy of In-service Training courses. Data were collected with the help of this instrument from the Teacher Educators associated with planning and organization of various In-service Training Programmes by the DIETs and ST schools. Besides, first-hand information was collected from the respondents on different courses, duration and objectives, course content and deficiencies felt by them in organization of course. Suggestions were invited from them about inclusion of items felt desirable by them. Advice was also sought from them on duration, resource persons, methods adopted and use of AV aids for improving the teaching-learning process.

4.8 COLLECTION OF DATA

The lists of Teacher Educators of different DIETs and ST schools were collected from SCERT, Bhubaneswar, Orissa. Then the data collection was made from the Teacher Educators of DIETs and ST Schools, mainly through personal contact.

Before going through the **Teacher Educator Data Form,** Teacher Educators were requested to give their natural, free and frank responses to the items. They were taken into confidence and were told that the data provided by them would be used only for compilation and statistical analysis purely for research purpose and would be strictly kept secret.

In all, 544 Teacher Educators were given **'Teacher Educator Data Form'** with oral and written request. Some Teacher Educators held back the questionnaire and mailed it to the investigator or handed over the questionnaires to the Investigator personally. Some of them kept the questionnaires with them, but they did not return them in spite of several reminders from the Investigator. While collecting data from different DIETs and ST Schools, the Investigator was helped by the Heads of Institutes, Teacher Educators, students of DIETs and also by the non-teaching staff. Lastly, a total of 241 **Teacher Educator Data Forms** were received. Out of 241 questionnaires, 135 were received from DIETs and 106 were received from the Asst. teachers of ST Schools.

The personnel associated with Elementary Teacher Education Programme such as Headmasters of ST Schools, Principals of DIETs and experts in Education were individually interviewed by the investigator through a structured Opinionnaire (Appendix B). Each interviewee took about 1 to 1.5 hours for discussion. A good rapport was established with each interviewee. Only one question was asked at a time. Questions were repeated when required. The investigator made it sure that the interviewee understood all the questions put to him/her in proper perspective and listened carefully to the answers given by the interviewees allowing them sufficient time to answer to each question. The investigator conducted 30 such interviews and recorded the facts for evaluation.

The investigator also visited 24 ST schools and 11 DIETs to collect information from the records of the Institutions about the status with the help of an Observation Schedule (Appendix C). Again, 24 Asst. Teachers of ST Schools and 30 Teacher Educators from DIETs were Interviewed by the investigator to collect information about the In-service Training Programmes conducted in the

Institutes with the help of an Interview Schedule (Appendix D).

4.9 TABULATION OF DATA

For compilation of the collected data through Teacher Educator Data Form, Opinnionnare, Observation Schedule and Interview Schedule, tabulation sheets were prepared. Keeping in view the objectives spelt out and to compare the selected demographic, academic and professional characteristics of DIETs and ST Schools, the forms were first separated and then each item was compiled in the tabulation sheets.

4.10 ANALYSIS OF DATA

The data was then analysed keeping in view the objectives spelt out. The entire population was divided into two categories, i.e. DIETs and ST Schools. Then, the data of each item of the **Teacher Educator Data Form** has been presented in different tables and figure forms for facilitating analysis and interpretation. Likewise the data collected with the help of **Opinionnaire, Observation Schedule and Interview Schedule** were also computed, analysed and interpreted by calculating percentage.

Percentage, mean, Standard Deviation, T. tests were used to analyse the data.

5

Teacher Educators: Background and Characteristics

An attempt has been made in this chapter to critically examine and analyze the data collected from the relevant sets of respondents through appropriately designed instruments, such as questionnaire, interview schedule, and observation schedule. Analysis and interpretation constitutes the core of a research endeavour. A rich wealth of data continues to be a stockpile of information unless the data are insightfully analysed and meaningfully interpreted to draw evidence-based conclusions. To put it differently, analysis and interpretation seek to make the 'invisible', visible and the apparently 'meaningless' meaningful. Functionally, the purpose of analysis is to reduce data into meaningful and interpretable form, so that the relation of research problems can be studied and tested (Best 1993). Thus, analysis and interpretation is the most significant and useful step in educational research, which brings out results for taking up both short-term and long-term interventions in order to restructure and reform a system.

The analysis and interpretation of data, as attempted in this chapter, has focused on three significant aspects: (a) demographic characteristics, (b) academic background, and

(c) professional characteristics of Teacher Educators, the critical and key factors in the Teacher Education Institutions. The analysis of such data assumed further significance in consideration of the widely shared conviction that teachers' academic preparation and performance, professional attributes and demographic composition significantly contribute to the quality of schooling. In a broader perspective, the quality of teacher performance is largely a function of the quality and characteristics of Teacher Educators and Teacher Education Institutions. With the state of Orissa having, unlike many other Indian states, an exclusive Directorate for Teacher Education, its Teacher Education Institutions, both at the Elementary and Secondary stages, are expected to be at an advantage compared to those in other states. This overarching frame of reference informed the analysis attempted in this chapter.

A. DEMOGRAPHIC CHARACTERISTICS OF TEACHER EDUCATORS

Demographic characteristics such as age, sex, place of residence (rural/urban), caste, marital status, health and number of children, and some of the direct and indirect implications on effectiveness of Teacher Educators. Learning achievement is a function of time-on-task, i.e., academically engaged time or opportunity to learn. Some of the demographic variables noted above is likely to maximize time-on-task. The following sub-sections are devoted to an analysis on the demographic characteristics of Teacher Educators working in two different sets of Elementary Teacher Education Institutions, viz. ST Schools and DIETs.

5.1 TEACHER EDUCATORS BY AGE

Table 5.1 presents the distribution of Teacher Educators by their chronological age.

The following picture, with regard to age-composition by sex, is evident from the figures furnished in the Table 5.1.

- Male Teacher Educators out-number female Teacher Educators both in DIETs and STSs. This male advantage is a typical characteristic of the

TABLE 5.1

Distribution of Teacher Educators by Age

Age range	DIETs			STSs.		
	Male	Female	Total	Male	Female	Total
55-59	19 (14.1)	05 (3.7)	24 (17.8)	14 (13.2)	02 (1.9)	16 (15.1)
50-54	10 (7.4)	09 (6.7)	19 (14.1)	12 (11.3)	05 (4.7)	17 (16.0)
45-49	06 (4.4)	07 (5.2)	13 (9.6)	17 (16.0)	05 (4.7)	22 (20.7)
40-44	18 (13.3)	10 (7.4)	28 (20.7)	11 (10.4)	04 (3.8)	15 (14.2)
35-39	16 (11.9)	06 (4.4)	22 (16.3)	10 (9.4)	03 (2.8)	13 (12.2)
30-34	12 (8.9)	03 (2.2)	15 (11.1)	13 (12.3)	02 (1.9)	15 (14.2)
25-29	10 (7.4)	04 (3.0)	14 (10.4)	07 (6.6)	01 (0.9)	08 (7.5)
Total	91 (67.4)	44 (32.6)	135 (100)	84 (79.2)	22 (20.8)	106 (100)

Note: Figures within ( ) represent percentages.

teaching workforce across all sectors of education in the state. However, the present position with regard to representation of women in the teaching workforce is a significant improvement over the position that was obtained during 1980s and 1990s.

- In a comparative perspective, while female Teacher Educators constitute almost one-third (32.6%) of the teaching workforce in DIETs, the proportion of female Teacher Educators in STSs is a one-fifth (20.8%). The percentage of female Teacher Educators in STSs is highly inconsistent as there exists no direct recruitment in STSs. Such TEs belong to the Junior Secondary Education Service (JSES) cadre and placed in STSs on transfer basis as and when required. The relative advantage of female TEs in DIETs is partly due to reservation of posts for women candidates and availability of larger number of female candidates with MA (Education) or M.Ed. This proportion (32.6%) of female TEs in DIETs has remained almost constant since 1989-90 with no recruitment till 1996-97.

- Male and female TEs, taken together, constitute the largest single chunk (20.7%) of TEs of the age-group 40-44, representing a little over one-fifth of TEs in DIETs. A similar percentage (20.7%) of Teacher Educators of STSs belong to the next higher age-bracket, i.e., 45-49. A little over half (51.8%) of the teaching corps of STSs is above 45 years of age. The percentage of TEs aged 45+ in DIETs, on the other hand, is a little over two-fifths (41.5%) of the total TEs. This difference is possibly due to the fact that senior teachers of Secondary Education cadre prefer, once placed in STSs, to stay back and retire in that position from service.
- The percentages of young TEs, in DIETs as well as in STSs, is very insignificant, 10.4 in DIETs and 7.5 in STSs. Low proportion of such TEs in DIETs is primarily due to non-recruitment of TEs since 1997, and the first spell of recruitment of TEs in DIETs was made in 1989-90. In case of STSs, young teachers, when recruited, are swayed away by their desire and drive to teach young and ebullient school children. The near absence of the youth in the teaching workforce in TEIs has academic implications.
- The percentages of TEs who are in the twilight zone of their retirement, i.e. in the age-bracket of 55-59, are 17.8 in DIETs and 15.1 in STSs. While their long experience is an advantage, physical fatigue and exhaustion stands to be a constraint.

5.2 TEACHER EDUCATORS BY SEX

In the DIETs, male Teacher Educators constituted 67 percent and Female Teacher Educators 33 percentage, while in ST schools the male and female counterparts constituted 79 percent and 21 per cent respectively. It was not corresponding to the male-female ratio of the Orissa population (Census 2001).

5.3 TEACHER EDUCATORS BY RELIGION

TEs in DIETs as well as in STSs are predominantly Hindus: 97.8 per cent in DIETs and 100 per cent in STSs. Christians, mostly Tribal converts, constitute about 1.5 per cent of TEs in position. This position is by accident, not on account of any policy decision. Even though a TE's religion does not have any relationship with his/her performance, observations make it evident that Tribals, who enter the teaching profession through the mechanism of affirmative action, are almost without exception, known for their mediocre academic achievement and performance.

5.4 CASTE COMPOSITION OF TEACHER EDUCATORS

Caste-based reservation for appointment to posts is constitutionally mandated in India. This, as an affirmative action, is intended to neutralize the historical disadvantages the people of 'lower' castes in the Indian caste hierarchy have been subjected to Table 5.2 depicts the composition of TEs in DIETs and STSs by major class clusters .

TABLE 5.2

Composition of Teacher Educators by Castes

Castes	*DIETs*	*STSs*
Scheduled Caste	08 (5.92)	04 (3.78)
Scheduled Tribe	11 (8.15)	05 (4.71)
Other Backward Class	38 (28.15)	24 (22.64)
General	78 (57.78)	73 (68.87)
Total	135(100.00)	106(100.0)

Note: Figures within ( ) represent percentages.

- Teacher Educators of the scheduled population, viz. Scheduled Castes and Scheduled Tribes, and other Backward Classes (OBCs)/Socio-economically Backward Classes (SEBC) constitute 37.3 per cent in DIETs and STSs taken together.

Break-up of the caste composition separately, caste-wise and institution category-wise, presents different configurations.

- Teacher Educators of the Scheduled Caste category constitute only 5.9 and 3.8 per cent of the total Teacher Educators in DIETs and STs schools respectively as against an earmarked 16 per cent reservation in jobs for this caste category. In other words, SC caste category is grossly under-represented, which has its own educational implications. While abysmally low representation of SCs in STSs is due to indiscriminate placement of TEs from the Secondary Education cadre, their under-representation in DIETs is probably due to the non-availability of eligible candidates with NCTE prescribed qualifications, i.e. Master's Degree in a School subject with Masters Degree in Education. This is a glaring case of supply side deficit.
- A similar position obtains with regard to Teacher Educators of ST category. Overall, this group comprises only 6.6 per cent in DIETs and STSs, taken together. The position is relatively better in DIETs (8.2%) than STSs (4.7%). Like the under-representation of SC category TEs, the under-representation of ST Teacher Educators is largely due to supply side deficit.
- Teacher Educators of OBC/SEBC category costitute 28.2 per cent in DIETs and 22.6 per cent in STSs. This position is roughly in consonance with the proportion (27%) of the caste category in the overall population of the state.
- Teacher Educators of the 'unreserved' category dominate the teaching workforce: their overall percentage being 62.7%. This cluster comprises upper caste people with leverages of caste hierarchy and caste-based entitlements.

The unacceptably low proportion of TEs of SC and ST category, despite constitutionally committed affirmative action tends to affect education of student-teachers of TEIs. The persistence of the old notion that education is not important for members of the "lower castes" has still its hold in the mind-set of policy-makers, which invisibly affects the strength of public commitment to the promotion of education among these historically disadvantaged groups Dreze and Sen (1995). The under-representation of SCs and STs in the teaching workforce in Elementary Teacher Education Institutions, notwithstanding their relative share of 17.8 and 22.2 per cent in the total population of the State (Census 2001), is a cause for concern, requiring probably appropriate affirmative action in order to redress the still evasive disadvantages.

This aside, the DIETs in the State have been grouped as, 'Tribal and Non-tribal', based on their location in districts perhaps with an intended positive discriminatory perspective for the development of these 'scheduled' category student-teachers and primary school children.

5.5 RURAL-URBAN BACKGROUND OF TEACHER EDUCATORS

The distribution of TEs by their rural-urban background has been presented in Table 5.3 below:

TABLE 5.3

Rural-Urban Distribution of Teacher Educators

Rural/Urban	*DIETs*	*STSs*
Rural	99 (73.0)	84 (79.0)
Urban	36 (27.0)	22 (21.0)
Total	135 (100.0)	106 (100.0)

Note: Figures within ( ) represent percentages.

The following position is evident from the figures furnished in the Table 5.3.

- Overall, more than three-fourths (76%) of Teacher Educators of DIETs and STSs are of rural origin, which is characteristic of the rural-urban divide of the State, i.e. Orissa is predominantly a State with high percentage (Census 2001) of rural population.

- Percentages of Teacher Educators with urban origin in DIETs and STSs are 27.0 and 21.0 respectively.

The rural origin and thereby, their intimate acquaintance with the ground realities in which education of rural children takes place aid them to negotiate their teaching effectively, taking cognisance of local diversities.

5.6 HEALTH STATUS OF TEACHER EDUCATORS

Sound physical health is an essential condition for working with effectiveness. Poor or failing health on the part of teachers leads to frequent absence, authorized or unauthorized, resulting in loss of instructional hours, i.e., reduced time-on-task. Besides, poor health and poor mental health very often co-exist. Poor health affects teachers' effectiveness and productivity.

The health status of Teacher Educators, as assessed by themselves, is presented in Table 5.4

TABLE 5.4

Health Status of Teacher Educators

Health Status	*DIETs*	*STSs*
Excellent	18(13.3)	14(13.2)
Good	42(31.1)	32(30.2)
Average	75(55.6)	60(56.6)
Total	135(100.0)	106(100.0)

Note: Figures within ( ) represent percentages.

From the Table, it is evident that:

- Only a minuscule number of TEs have reported that they possessed "excellent" health. In terms of percentage, it is as low as 13.3 in DIETs and 13.2 in STSs.

- Less than one-third of TEs said to have 'good' physical health: 31.1 per cent in DIETs and 30.2 per cent in STSs.
- "Average" health is reported to be possessed by more than 55.0 per cent of Teacher Educators. This 'average' health status possibly conceals "poor" health. The incidence of "average" health, with hidden 'poor' health is quite disquieting with serious implications for effective teaching. This affects the performance and professional commitment of Teacher Educators.

5.7 MARITAL STATUS OF TEACHER EDUCATORS

Table below presents the marital status of Teacher Educators of TEIs of the state. Marital status, either married or unmarried, has its own implications for Teacher Educators as professionals. The following picture emerges with regard to the marital status of Teacher Educators of DIETs and STSs.

TABLE 5.5

Marital Status of Teacher Educators

Marital Status	*DIETs*	*STSs*	*Overall*
Unmarried	28 (20.7)	16 (15.0)	44 (18.26)
Married	106 (78.6)	85 (80.0)	191 (79.25)
Separated	01 (0.7)	05 (05.0)	06 (2.49)
Divorced	Nil (0.0)	Nil (0.0)	Nil (0.0)
Total	135(100.0)	106 (100.0)	241 (100.00)

Note: Figures within ( ) represent percentages.

- Married Teacher Educators constitute a majority, i.e. a little less than four-fifths (79.25%) of TEs. Broken down to DIETs and STSs separately, the respective percentages are 78.6 and 80.0. The proportion of married TEs in STSs outstrips that of DIETs. This could be accounted for by: first, higher percentage of TEs in DIETs of the 25-29 age-group (10.4), compared to 8.0 percent in STSs, who are possibly yet to enter wed-lock; and second, more women TEs in DIETs, who are usually found to be spinsters for various reasons.

- Conversely, the percentages of unmarried TEs are 20.7 per cent in DIETs and 15.0 per cent in STSs. Taken together, unmarried TEs comprise 18.26 per cent of the 241 TEs in position in DIETs and STSs.
- Separated and divorced among TEs are almost non-existent. This is essentially due to the culturally down-to-earth Oriya (people of Orissa) families, that have a rock-solid family bond. Rarely does one come across the incidence of divorce or separation, largely deterred by cultural norms and standards.

5.8 FAMILY SIZE OF TEACHER EDUCATORS

The picture of family (nucleus) size of TEs, in terms of the number of their offspring, has been prsented in Table 5.6.

TABLE 5.6

Number of Children of Teacher Educators

Number of Children	*DIETs*	*STSs*	*Overall*
None	34 (25.2)	26 (24.6)	60 (24.90)
1-2	62 (45.9)	35 (33.0)	97 (40.25)
3-4	26 (19.3)	33 (31.1)	59 (24.48)
5-6	12 (08.9)	10 (09.4)	22 (09.13)
More than 6	01 (0.7)	02 (01.9)	03 (01.24)
Total	135(100.0)	106(100.0)	241(100.0)

Note: Figures within ( ) represent percentages.

A perceptive look at the contents of the Table makes the following evident:

- Overall. almost one-fourth (24.9%) of TEs arefound to have no offspring, possibly, they are of the young age-group, married a couple of years back or still unmarried.
- TEs, with one to two children, considered small family norm in India, constitute 45.9 percent in DIETs and 33.0 per cent in STSs, the average for both being 40.25 per cent. Comparatively the percentage of TEs, with "observance of small family norm" in STSs is significantly less than that of TEs in DIETs.
- Correspondingly, the percentage of TEs in STSs with three-to-four children is much higher (31.1%), compared to only 19.3 per cent in case of TEs in DIETs.
- TEs, with five-to-six children in DIETs and STSs, constitute an almost equal percentage: 8.9 per cent in DIETs and 9.4 per cent in STSs.

The larger the family size, the greater is likely to be the family commitments, which tend to deflect teachers' commitment to teaching. TEs, burdened with family responsibilities, find it difficult to pursue academic excellence. To put it differently, family commitments tend to affect professional commitments.

To sum up, demographic variables such as age composition, rural-urban divide, caste, marital status, and family size do, directly or indirectly, impact professional performance of teachers. These variables impact one's performance with variations.

B. ACADEMIC BACKGROUND OF TEACHER EDUCATORS

Evidence-based researches and common experience suggest that one's academic preparation, pursuits for teaching and research, attitude towards continued self-development, and participation in interactive seminars and consultations impact one's performance as a teacher or Teacher Educator. Good teachers certainly make a difference. This difference gets manifested in the presage, process and product variables. The present section makes an attempt to examine the academic background and other correlated characteristics of TEs working in the Elementary Teacher Education Institutions of Orissa. The analysis is based on data collected from the Teacher Educators and the Teacher Education Institutions.

5.9 ACADEMIC QUALIFICATIONS OF TEACHER EDUCATORS

A good teacher, almost universally conceded, knows both John and Latin. S/he intimately knows, among other things, the child and the myriad ways by which it learns, the context in which it learns, the stuff to be taught and the teaching strategies. All these are developed by his/her academic and professional preparation. Table 5.7 presents academic background of Teacher Educators.

TABLE 5.7

Academic Qualifications of Teacher Educators

Type of Institution	*B.A.*	*B.Sc.*	*M.A.*	*M.Sc.*	*M.Phil.*	*Ph.D.*	*B.Ed.*	*M.Ed.*
DIETs	30	11	76	16	17	08	51	64
	(22)	(08)	(56)	(12)	(13)	(06)	(38)	(47)
STSs	37	18	26	04	Nil	Nil	60	25
	(35)	(17)	(25)	(03)	-	-	(57)	(23)

Note: Figures within ( ) represent percentages.

The DIET Guidelines (Government of India 1989) and the National Council for Teacher Education (Ministry of Human Resources Department, Government of India), 1995 have a set of prescribed qualifications for appointment to faculty positions in DIETs. The NCTE prescribed qualifications are also mandatory for Secondary or

Elementary Training Schools that offer the two-year Elementary Teacher Training course. The Gazette of India: Extraordinary, Part-III, Section-IV, 5-b the minimum qualification of Teacher Educator (Lecturer) in Elementary Teacher Education programme should have good academic record with M.Ed./M.A. (Education) with 55% marks, preferably with specialisation in Elementary Education or good academic record with Master's degree with 55% marks in the relevant school subject and Bachelor of Elementary Education (B.El. Ed.) or B.Ed. preference with specialisation in Elementary Education, and with five years teaching experience in recognised elementary schools. These qualifications have been prescribed for maintenance of standard and excellence in Elementary Teacher Education Institutions.

Analysis of data furnished in Table 5.7 makes the following evident:

- Ph.D. and M.Phil. Degree in Education, considered specialized qualification, is barely possessed by Teacher Educators. Only six percent of Teacher Educators of DIETs possessed Ph.D. Degree, whereas 13 per cent possessed M.Phil. Degree. It is found that those who possessed Ph.D. Degree, they did it while in service, which evinces their genuine pursuit to upgrade their qualifications. Lack of such self-motivated inerest conspicuous in case of majority of Teacher Educators.
- The number of Teacher Educators with Science background is very few: in terms of percentages TEs with B.Sc. and M.Sc. qualifications in DIETs are only 17 and 12 respectively. The corresponding percentages in ST Schools being 17 and 3 only. This low percentage of TEs with Science background is due primarily to indiscriminate recruitment of TEs, regardless of the requirement to teach different subjects and methodology of teaching. The dearth of TEs with Science background affects teaching of Science and Mathematics content as well as methodology

- Qualification-wise, STSs are at a major disadvantage. Most of the TEs in STSs are not in possession of Government of India or NCTE prescribed qualifications. Therefore, quality of instruction in STSs, reckoned by all parameters, is substantially inferior to that of in DIETs. The quality gets further exacerbated by the non-availability of essential instructional and infrastructural facilities.
- Another disquieting phenomenon is that those Teacher Educators in ST Schools, who are deficient in possession of essential qualifications, and desire to continue there, do not evince any interest to upgrade their qualifications. This affects their performance and productivity as TEs. Absence of a common cadre for Teacher Educators of DIETs and STSs perhaps act as a deterrent for upgrading their qualifications.

5.10 ROLE PREFERENCE OF TEACHER EDUCATORS

Teaching, research and extension are considered to be the prime functions of Teacher Education Institutions. TEs of DIETs and STSs were asked to indicate their relative role preference for teaching and research in terms of five preferences viz. predominantly teaching, predominantly research, both teaching and research but leaning towards teaching, teaching and research equally and teaching and research but leaning towards research, Table 5.8 presents the preferences of Teacher Educaors of DIETs and STSs.

The following picture emerges from the analysis of the contents of the Table 5.8:

- Teaching is found to be most preferred role of TEs of both DIETs and STSs. Sixty per cent of TEs of DIETs and 82.0 per cent of TEs of STSs registered their strong preference (heavily and leaning towards teaching) for teaching. Higher percentage of TEs of STSs with stronger preference for teaching. It reflects their of art: almost total

TABLE 5.8

Relative Role Preference of Teacher Educators

Role Preference	*DIETs Nos.*	*STSs Nos.*
Very heavily in teaching	37(27.0)	52(49.0)
In both but learning towards teaching	45(33.0)	35(33.0)
In both equally	30(22.0)	12(11.0)
In both, but learning towards research	16(12.0)	05(5.0)
Very heavily in research	07(06.0)	02(2.0)
Total	135(100.0)	106(100.0)

Note: Figures within ( ) represent percentages.

absence of state climate for research in STSs. This could be attributed to: first, non-availability of TEs with MEd or MA (Education) who have been oriented in research methodology; second, STSs have been functioning in the traditional mode of training for teaching, research gets no premium in the scheme of things in STSs; and third, rarely do heads of STSs provide space for research in the curriculum structure possibly informed by the myth that research is the exclusive preserve of the institutions of higher education.

- Even though DIETs have been conceived in a broader perspective with research and innovation over arching their programmes and activities, research does not receive the emphasis as expected. This is evident from the role preference of TEs reflected in the Table coupled with other evidence-based indicators such as publication of research-based papers by TEs. Preference for research by TEs of DIETs is shown by a bare less than one-fifth (18.0%). This is an unacceptable position despite the importance attached to researches on primary education in DPEP/SSA. This reflects, to a large measure, the absence of a broad base for research and leadership in DIETs.

The position gets strengthened further by the results of the chi-square test as reflected in Table 5.9.

TABLE 5.9

Contingency Table for Chi-Square Test of Independence between the Role Preference of Teacher Educator's and Type of Institutions

Role Preference	*DIETs*	*STSs*	*Total*
Very heavily in teaching	37 (49.85)	52 (39.15)	89
In both, but learning towards teaching	45 (44.81)	35 (35.19)	80
In both equally	30 (23.53)	12 (18.47)	42
In both, but learning towards research	16 (11.76)	05 (09.24)	21
Very heavily in research	07(05.04)	02 (03.96)	09
Totals	135	106	241

Note: Figures within ( ) represent percentages.
$X^2 = 16.784$ df = 4.
Significant at 0.01 level.

5.11 PUBLICATIONS BY TEACHER EDUCATORS

Publications, more particularly research-based and reflective reflect the academic excellence and interest of Teacher Educators. Table 5.10 presents the number and percentages of TEs who have published articles in different magazines and journals. The number of published articles/ papers, without being qualified with regard to their category, quality and journals in which published, imposes limitations on attempting an in-depth analysis. The following position obtains from the data furnished in the Table 5.10.

- A predominantly large proportion of TEs, both in DIETs and STSs, do not have a single publication to their credit. The percentages are unacceptably high: it is 83 per cent in DIETs and still higher (92%)in STSs.

TABLE 5.10

Distribution of Articles Published

No. of Articles Published	*DIETs Nos.*	*STSs Nos.*
None	112 (83.0)	98 (92.4)
1-5	16 (11.8)	06 (05.7)
6-10	05 (03.7)	02 (01.9)
More than 10	02 (01.5)	Nil (Nil)
Total	135(100)	106(100)

Note: Figures within ( ) represent precent.

- In terms of number of articles published by TEs, percentage of TEs with more than 10 publications is a meagre one per cent in DIETs (Two out of 136). Considered from the point of view of their continued service in DIETs over at least a decade, the number is deplorably low. This reflects, in a way, lack of serious reflection on the part of the TEs and the absence of an incentive mechanism in the system for career advancement. Even the percentage of TEs who have published 1 to 5 articles is only 12 which, by all standards, is very low.
- In respect of TEs of STSs, the position is very discouraging. Only eight TEs out of 106 in STSs have published articles, which works out to be only 7.5 per cent.
- This very bleak picture speaks loudly of the extent and quality of academic pursuits of TEs of Elementary Teacher Education Institutions.

5.12 PRESENTATION OF PAPERS IN THE SEMINARS AND CONSULTATION AT THE STATE AND NATIONAL LEVEL

Presentation of papers in the State and National level seminars and consultations is considered prestigious, and represents the academic standard and rigor of TEs. Only those who are seriously involved in academic reflection, develop papers and present them in seminars and consultations. Developing and presenting papers also reflect individual and collective creativity, vision and ideas at the level of TEIs. This action tends to have demonstration effects on the other colleagues.

TABLE 5.11

Presentation of Papers in the Sate and National Level Seminars and Consultations

Number of seminars or Consultations	*At state level*		*Number of Seminar or Consultations*	*At National level*	
	DIETs Nos.	*STs Nos.*		*DIETs Nos.*	*STSs Nos.*
None	105(78)	96(90)	None	121(90)	104(98)
1-5	25(19)	07(07)	1-3	12(09)	02(02)
6-10	03(02)	02(02)	4-6	02(01)	Nill
11-15	02(01)	01(01)	7-9	Nil	Nill
Total	135(100)	106(100)	Total	135(100)	106(100)

Note: Figures within ( ) represent percentages.

The analysis brings out the following facts:

- Despite quite a large number of seminars and consultations on critical concerns in primary education organized at the state and national levels, presentation of papers by the faculty of TEIs is found to be very negligible. In terms of numbers and percentages, the extent of presentation of papers is at a very low ebb. Only 22.2 per cent of TEs have presented papers at the state level seminars, the number of papers presented ranges from 1 to 15, 1 to 5 constituting a sizable segment. The corresponding figure at the national level is found to be a bare 10.0 precent, with only two TEs presenting papers ranging from 6 to 10. The position in respect of ST Schools is evidently depressing. Only two TEs out of total of 106, have presented papers at the national level seminars.

- Conversely, the percentages of TEs of DIETs and ST Schools who have not presented even a single paper at the State and National level seminars are: DIETs (78.0, 90.0) and ST Schools (90.0, 98.0).
- Those TEs who presented papers were almost certainly self-propelled, Institutional and collegial encouragement is almost non-existent. This aside, as common observation testifies, an identified small group of TEs presented papers.

5.13 HOBBIES OF TEACHER EDUCATORS

TEs are found to have an extensive range of hobbies: from reading and listening to cooking, to social service. While some of the hobbies have direct or indirect bearing on their professional performance, others are discrete having no or remotest link with professional work. A few notable hobbies of TEs are as follows:

- Twenty-one percent of TEs of DIETs expressed that "reading" is their predominant hobby "reading" includes reading of newspapers, stories, novels and magazines.
- Thirteen per cent of TEs have participation in broadcasting, TV programmes and writing scripts for radio and TV as their hobby. Such TEs could possibly be effective in IT enabled instruction.
- Teacher Educators with "listening" as their hobby constituted about 15 per cent of the total TEs. The space of listening included: listening Radio and TV news, music and songs, others views, etc. Listening has enormous possibilities to make a good teacher: to listen to others with patience.
- A small segment of TEs, a little more than seven per cent, had "social service" caring for the diseased and the distressed, community mobilization for immunization, community and

school sanitation, social activism for restoring entitlements to the poor and the deprived, and mediating for the resolution of squabbles and conflicts at the village level.

- Eight per cent of TEs, mostly female, had cuisine as their hobby.
- The percentage of TEs with organization of co-curricular activities as their hobby was abysmally low: only four per cent. They are favourably inclined to organize different activities such as drama, annual functions, sports and picnics as a leader of co-functional teams. Such TEs organize institutional functions effectively and efficiently. Besides this, they have a propensity to conduct seminars, workshops and conferences, meetings, and various kinds of competitions among students. This hobby has a direct link with institutional functioning.

Teacher Educators' academic background and other attributes make them to be effective teachers. Some attributes have enabling impact, whereas some others constrain them to act proactively. Good teachers are good relation-builders. Quality of relationships is the most crucial element in children's learning.

C. PROFESSIONAL CHARACTERISTICS OF TEACHER EDUCATORS

Nature of work and working styles in Teacher Education Institutions differ markedly from that of institutions imparting general education. Regor of professional preparation and intimate student-teacher relationships TEIs distinguish them from others. This subsection deals with the professional activities of the Elementary Teacher Education Institutions in the State.

5.14 TEACHER EDUCATORS BY RANK

As stated earlier, DIETs and STSs constitute the

Elementary Teacher Education Institutions in the State. While DIETs are Centrally sponsored and almost entirely financed by the Government of India under Central Plan, STSs are under Non-Plan, being exclusively funded by the state Government. These two sets of institutions significantly differ from each other in respect of infrastructure, faculty, and academic climate. Besides, they differ functionally: DIETs have an extended role to play, whereas STSs have a singular conventional function, i.e., teaching. This variation is reflected in the faculty structure of DIETs and STSs.

The faculty structure of DIETs is dependent on the provisions of DIET Guidelines (GOI, 1989). The DIET faculty structure comprises a hierarchy consisting of Teacher Educators, Senior Teacher Educator and Principal. Out of a sample of 135, 34 were in the rank of Senior Teacher Educators, including six Vice-Principals, who are of the same rank. The senior most Senior Teacher Educator of DIET is designated as Vice-Principal. The prescribed faculty structure of a DIETs is, however, different: 14 TEs, seven STEs and a Principal. The present ratio of TEs and STEs is 4:1 against the ratio of 2:1. This STEs deficit is essentially because of non-promotion of TEs to the post of STE and no direct recruitment of STEs since 1989.

In STSs, the faculty structure is different. It consists of Assistant Teachers and Headmaster. They are from the secondary education cadre, put in STSs on transfer from secondary schools. STSs do not have a separate cadre. Nor do they have a common cadre with DIETs.

5.15 TEACHING EXPERIENCE

The composition of the faculty of ETEIs, split up into DIETs and STSs, according to experience has been presented in Table 5.12.

The following is evident from the Table 5.12:

- More than half (52%) of the TEs of DIETs are found to have five or less years of experience as Teacher Educators. One quarter of TEs had 6 to 10 years of experience. These TEs constituted a

TABLE 5.12

Distribution of Teacher Educators by Experience

Experience in Years	*Experience as* Teacher Educator DIET No.	STS No.	Lecturer DIET No.	STS No.	Teacher DIET No.	STS No.
5 or less	70 (51.9)	48 (45.3)	29 (21.5)	-	26 (19.3)	22 (20.8)
6 to 10	33 (24.4)	26 (24.5)	06 (04.4)	-	18 (13.3)	25 (23.6)
11 to 15	14 (10.4)	15 (14.2)	-	-	14 (10.4)	21 (19.8)
16 to 20	11 (08.1)	09 (08.5)	-	-	10 (07.4)	20 (18.9)
21 to 25	04 (03.0)	04 (03.8.)	-	-	11 (08.1)	10 (09.4)
26 to 30	03 (02.2)	04 (03.8.)	-	-	16 (11.9)	03 (02.8)
31 to 35	-	-	-	-	05 (03.7)	05 (04.7)
Total	135(100)	106 (100)	35 (25.9)	-	100(74.1)	106(100)

Note: Figures within ( ) represent percentages.

sizeable segment of Teacher Educators inducted into DIETs in the initial years, i.e., 1989-90 and 1991-92.

- Thirty five Teacher Educators, who were rehabilitated as TEs in DIETs, had worked in privately managed Teacher Training Colleges as Lecturers, with varying years of experiences (from five or less to 10 years), which were abolished by the State Government by an Ordinance in 1989. Similarly, about one-fifth (19.3%) of TEs, who were earlier secondary school teachers, have been working in DIETs with five or less years of experience. But ironically, teachers, from primary stream with GOI mandatory qualifications, have not been recruited to DIETs even though DIET Guidelines (1989) provides space for them. The provision for lateral entry, thus, is non-existent in the Teacher Education system in the State.
- Teacher Educators of ST Schools, with designation of Assistant Teachers, with six to 25 years of experience (both in Secondary Schools and STSs) constituted a large chunk (71%). Some of the

Assistant Teachers, once in STSs on transfer, preferred to stay back in STSs as they probably find it academically worth-staying.

- Wide variations in experience and varied background of TEs in DIETs could be accounted for the recruitment policy of the Department of School and Mass Education, Government of Orissa. The Personnel Policy (1990) of the State Government provides space for (i) Elementary School Teachers, (ii) Secondary School Teachers, (iii) candidates directly selected by the State Selection Board, (iv) candidates selected directly by the Directorate of Teacher Education and SCERT, (v) Lecturers of erstwhile Training Colleges under the private sector, and (vi) Post-Graduate Teachers of Post-Basic Schools, that were abolished in 1980s. This faculty-mix adds to the variations in experience and background of Teacher Educators.
- Experience acquired in Secondary Schools as teachers does aid such teachers as Teacher Educators in DIETs and STSs, in general teaching skills and competencies. Notwithstanding this experience, during initial years in TEIS, they find it difficult to negotiate the processes that call for different sets of skills to be effective. Teacher Educators with Training College experience find programmes in DIETs akin to those they have earlier been acquainted with as Lecturers. Nevertheless, training pupil-teachers for elementary schools requires some additional skills. Continuous in-service capacity building programmes compensates the skill deficit of such TEs.

5.16 TIME SPENT ON PERFORMING DIFFERENT ACTIVITIES

TEs in DIETs and STSs are required to carry out certain activities which generally include: (i) teaching, (ii) conducting training , (iii) supervising practice teaching lessons taken by pupil teachers, (iv) performing administrative work, and (v) doing action research. The distribution of time spent by TEs on these core activities has been reflected in Table 5.13.

An analysis of data furnished in Table 5.13 makes the following evident:

- A little more than one-third (35.6%) of TEs of DIETs and 31 per cent of TEs of STSs are found to have spent one to three hours per week on teaching. On the other extreme of the time-scale, it is found that more TEs of STSs spent more time on teaching: nearly one-third (30%) of TEs spent 10 to 12 hours per week as against 16.3 per cent of TEs in DIETs. This is possibly due to less number of TEs in STSs compared to those in DIETs.
- Conducting in-service training programmes for primary school teachers is a mandatory responsibility of DIETs for which GOI funds are made available to them through SCERT. More than two-fifths (40.7%) of TEs of DIETs spent 1 to 3 hours per week for taking training sessions. Next in order is the percentage (22.2) of TEs spending 7 to 9 hours per week. This variation is due to the number of programmes organized by DIETs and the size of faculty therein. The STSs, being funded by the state Government, are starved of funds for organizing in-service training programmes.
- Practice Teaching/internship is a core component of Teacher Education Programme. It is intended to equip the prospective teachers with a repertoire of pedagogical skills for effective classroom transaction. For this, the programme is expected to be more intensive and rigorous. It is found that 43.0 per cent of TEs in DIETs and 24.5 per cent of TEs in STSs devoted 1 to 3 hours per week to practice teaching. Common experience shows that time-on-task, i.e. real and effective time spent on

TABLE 5.13

Distribution of Time Spent on Different Activities

Time in Hours	*Regular Teaching*		*Conducting Training Prog.*		*Supervision in practice teaching*		*Administration*		*Action Research*	
	DIET No.	*STS No.*	*DIET No.*	*STS No.*	*DIET No.*	*STS No.*	*DIET No.*	*STS No.*	*DIET No.*	*STS No.*
1-3	48(35.6)	33(31.1)	55(40.7)	24(22.6)	58(43.0)	26(24.5)	36(26.7)	25(23.6)	42(31.1)	19(17.9)
4-6	40(29.6)	25(23.6)	26(19.3)	14(13.2)	20(14.8)	19(17.9)	26(19.2)	23(21.7)	12(8.9)	—
7-9	25(18.5)	16(15.1)	30(22.2)	12(11.3)	16(11.8)	12(11.3)	27(20.0)	—	08(5.9)	—
10-12	22(16.3)	32(30.2)	24(17.8)	13(12.3)	15(11.1)	18(17.0)	05(3.7)	23(21.7)	05(3.7)	—
Total	135(100)	106(100)	135(100)	63(59.4)	109(80.7)	75(70.7)	94(69.6)	71(67.0)	67(49.5)	19(17.9)

Note: Figures within ( ) represent percentages.

supervision of lessons taught by pupil-teachers is substantially less, compared to the time said to have been spent by TEs. The 'invisible' time lost is a greater than the 'apparent' time spent on supervision.

- School heads viz. Principals/Vic-principals in DIETs and Headmasters in STSs are specifically in position for day-to-day management of the institutions. Non-positioning of institutional heads entails additional responsibilities on Teacher Educators. Around one-fourth of TEs spent 1 to 3 hours per week for administration in DIETs (26.7%) and STSs (23.6%). Higher proportion of teachers spending time on day-to-day management of DIETs is primarily due to: first, their diversified programmes; second, up-down and bottom-up flow of compliance reports; third, DPEP/SSA assignments entrusted to them; fourth, admission to the course each year. The TEs of STSs are saddled with administrative work due primarily to non-placement of headmasters. In a sense, the time spent on administrative, work is instruction supportive not time taken away from the core functions of TEIs. In an educational Institution work is predominantly academic.
- As mentioned earlier in this chapter, undertaking action research has not been given the premium in TEIs as ought to have been Action research as widely known as "research by practioners" substantially aids TEs and teachers, in turn, to perform their mandated task. Low priority given to action research even in DIETs, a new generation TEIs, is evident enough from the amount of time (1 to 3 hours/pw) given to action research by less than one-third (31.1%) of TEs. Even this appears to be on the higher side when their role perception is considered.

5.17 IN-SERVICE TRAINING PROGRAMMES

To compensate for teachers' limited subject knowledge and repertoire of teaching practices, both the Central and State Governments, have supported the development of in-service teacher training. The programmes, mostly centrally (GOI) funded, are intended to (i) improve and upgrade subject knowledge, (ii) change teaching practices, and (iii) acquaint teachers with new and emerging concerns considered to be essential for teachers. However, what matters most is the quality of such programmes and the extent to which they impact teacher's classroom practices. National and international experience with teacher training suggests that its impact is a function of the quality and relevance, duration, timing, strategies, location of training venues, and monitoring.

This sub-section discusses the in-service training programmes organized, areas/themes of such programmes, duration, and the agency/institution that organized such programmes.

5.17.1 Induction and Orientation Courses

The data relating to induction and orientation courses organized for the DIET faculty have been presented in Table 5.14.

The following picture emerges:

- The Directorate of Teacher Education and SCERT, Orissa conducted the induction level training for TEs of DIETs as late as in the year 2000, precisely, after almost a decade after DIETs got established and TEs inducted into the system. As required, this would have been organized immediately after the TEs were put in position in DIETs. One of the weaknesses of this programme was that the fresh TEs of STSs appointed a fresh or posted on transfer, were not covered. To be more effective, this five-day course could have been followed by periodic reinforcement to sustain changes in teaching behaviour and to be conversant with the

TABLE 5.14

Profile of Programmes on Induction and Orientation for Teacher Educators

Sl. No.	*Courses*	*Teachers Educators attended*		*Content*	*Duration*	*Organized by*	*Any follow-up*
		DIETs No.	*STSs No.*				
1.	Induction level	135(100.0)	-	Introduction of Different dept. of New programmes	5 days	SCERT	Nil
2.	SOPT	135(100.0)	27(25.5)	Operation Black Board School Readness, Multigrade teaching, Education for Girls. Physically handicapped, Art & Aesthetic Morale Education.	7 days	SCERT	Nil
3.	MLL	45(33.3)	30(28.3)	What, Why & How MLL, Competency MLL, Math, EVs.	5 days	SCERT	Nil

Note: Figures within ( ) represent precentages.

expanded roles of DIETs, as mandated by emerging developments. The absence of follow-up and on-site support largely tended to neutralize the gains acquired.

- Special Orientation Programme for Teachers (SOPT) in the aftermath of the National Policy on Education (1986), one of the largest in-service programmes by states for Teacher Educators to act as Resource Persons was attended by all TEs of DIETs and one-quarter selected TEs of STSs. In terms of duration, it was appropriate. However, the enormity of the programme for teachers that followed rendered monitoring difficult and daunting. Again, SOPT was not followed by short duration courses.
- Orientation courses on Minimum Levels of Learning (MLL) during 1990s were attended by 33 percent TEs of DIETs and nearly 28.0 per cent of TEs of STSs. It was a Unicef-supported programme on competence-based teaching, teaching-learning materials, and learner evaluation. The absence of follow-up mechanism made such programmes rarely effective.

To sum up, these programmes were not planned appropriately in terms of their design, duration, place of training, process of delivery, follow-up mechanisms and monitoring for effective no-site academic support. The relative neglect of a set of Elementary Teacher Education Institutions, viz. STSs, which outnumber DIETs both interms of their numbers and intake of pre-service students, worked as a major disadvantage for quality primary education in the State. Added to this, in-service teacher training is rarely conducted well (World Bank, 1997). Active learning, application to classroom practices, regular follow-up, and action research are key to improving transmission and sustaining change. These were largely missing in STSs.

5.17.2 Workshops

Workshops were organized for development of training

packages on three important areas: activity-based teaching-learning, alternative schooling (alternative schools are meant for disadvantaged children who cannot attend full-time mainstream formal schools), and joyful-learning, an initiative by the Unicef. These workshops were organized under the auspices of District Primary Education Programme and Education for All. The extent of participation by TEs in these workshops has been presented in Table 5.15

Analysis of the data presented in the Table 5.15 reveals that:

- On a very limited scale, Teacher Educators of DIETs participated in these workshops. In terms of number and percentages, participation ranges from 8 to 10 TEs and about 6 to 7 per cent of TEs. This very low level of participation was on account of: first, DPEP and EFA were in their nascent stage with low-key activities; second, for ensuring quality of materials only, an identified small group of competent TEs was involved in the development of materials, and third, a small core group was trained at the national level to be assigned with the task of preparing materials. This pool of core Resource Persons was found expanded later to cope with the increased scale and heightened intensity of DPEP and EFA activities.
- Non-involvement of TEs of STSs in these workshops was primarily due to the priority accorded to DIETs as district level centers of excellence. In addition, Resource Persons with competence were rarely found in STSs with national level exposure.
- Like capacity building programmes, there existed no mechanism for follow-up to effect the process of mid-course corrections and modifications of materials developed in workshop.

5.17.3 Distance Education

Distance Education is a form of IT-aided education

TABLE 5.15

Distribution of Workshops

Sl. No.	Name of the workshop	No. and % of Teacher Educators attended		Content	Duration	Organized by	Any follow-up
		DIET No.	STS No.				
1.	Preparation of training module						
	(a) On activity-based approach	8 (6.0)	—	Understand the Child, how Children learn.	7 days	DPEP	Nil
	(b) Alternative schools	10 (7.0)	—	preparation of Activity in different Subjects importance to AS.	7 days	DPEP	Nil
	(c) Joyful learning	8 (6.0)	—	Develop of TLM Preparatiion of Activity in different Subjects (Language, Math, Evs, Science)	7 days	EFA	Nil

Note: Figures within ( ) represent percentages.

with an expanded outreach and enriched qualitative inputs. DPEP made use of this cost-effective mode to help teachers and Block level supervisors such as, Block Resource Groups. In order to strengthen the distance education mode, GOI opened a Unit in the Indira Gandhi National Open University, known as DEP-DPEP. Each State DPEP Project Office had also a Distance Education Unit, funded exclusively by GOI.

State level DEP and national level DEP-DPEP conducted a series of programmes for creating a Resource Person pool to carry out the activities of the DEP. DIET faculty were involved in a limited extent in such programmes. This is evident from the figures furnished in Table 5.16.

DEP-DPEP spectrum of programmes included two major activities: (i) script writing for TV/Radio broadcast and books on hard spots in Language, Maths and Science; and (ii) Teleconferencing for Block Resource Groups for clarification of doubts and problem resolution. The following picture emerges:

Extent of participation of DIET faculty in these programmes was found to be extremely limited. Only 13 out of 135 TEs, i.e., 10 per cent of TEs participated in script writing for TV/Radio broadcast. Still less in Teleconferencing and writing of books on hardspots in Language, Maths and Science—a bare four per cent.

Follow-up work was conspicuously absent rendering such programmes of limited effectiveness. Absence of follow-up mechanism, common to almost all programmes, was one of the major deficiencies.

TEs of STSs were not involved in the DEP-DPEP. STSs have, like DIETs, a few potential TEs whose services could have been utilized for distance education programme. Such Teacher Educators need to be identified through appropriate means. The participation needs to be broad-based.

5.17.4 Methods and Techniques of Teaching

Mathematics, Science and English are the four core subjects taught in primary classes. With the up-gradation of content in these subjects, primary school teachers with class

TABLE 5.16

Distribution of Training Programmes in Distance Education

Sl. No.	Name of the Training Prorammes	No. and % of Teacher Educators attended		Content	Duration	Organized by	Any follow-up
		DDIETs No.	STSs No.				
1.	Script Writing						
	(a) TV and Radio	13 (9.6)	—	Math, Lang. and	7 days	DEP	Nil
	Programme		—	Science		DPEP	Nil
	(b) Ekalabya			Hard spots in		DEP	
	(Book)	5 (3.7)	—	Science, Math, & Lang.	7 days	DPEP	Nil
2.	Teleconference	5 (3.7)	—	Problem faced by BRG (Block Resource group in different DPEP	2 days	IGNOU Delhi	Nil

Note: Figures within ( ) represent percentages.

10 pass qualification find it extremely difficult to teach. In the absence of subject teachers, task of teaching becomes still more challenging, particularly at the upper primary level, i.e., classes VI and VII. Keeping this in view, SCERT conducted a few programmes for TEs who would, in turn, train primary school teachers.

The extent of participation of DIET faculty in such programmes is presented in Table 5.17

The following facts stand out from the Table 5.17

- The capacity building programmes focused on difficult concepts in three subject areas. The concepts covered were identified through diagnostic tests administered to primary school teachers who were expected to teach all subjects in a particular class. With no specialization in teaching of a subject, many teachers have little understanding of the material they teach. Significant deficits in teachers' knowledge of Mathematics and Environmental Studies (Science) is common.
- Twenty-eight per cent of Teacher Educators with Science and Mathematics background participated in the programmes on Science Teaching. The corresponding percentage for Mathematics teaching was only 15 per cent. Low proportion of TEs with BSc/MSc qualification and dearth of TEs in general explain the limited participation of TEs of DIETs. Converted to percentage to the TEs with Science background, the percentage of TEs shall be higher. The SCERT conducted one programme each in these subjects.
- English is a difficult subject to be taught in primary schools. Teachers' subject knowledge deficit in English is widely recognized. Therefore, English is poorly taught at the lower level. A selected group of 20 TEs, constituting only 15 per cent, participated in the course.
- All these programmes were organized by SCERT. Without exception, there existed no follow-up mechanism to ascertain the extent of transmission and sustenance for corrective action.

TABLE 5.17

Participation of Teacher Educators in Capacity Building Programme

Sl. No.	Name of the Course	No. and % of Teacher Educators attended		Content	Duration	Organized by	Any follow-up
		DDIETs No.	STSs No.				
1.	Science Teaching	38 (28.1)	7 (6.6)	New areas—Work Energy power, Cell Structure, System of the body, Evaluation	5 days	SCERT	Nil
2.	Math Teaching	20 (14.8)	4 (3.8)	Set theory, Profit & Loss, Methods of teaching, Content analysis, Evaluation.	5 days	SCERT	Nil
3.	English Teaching	20 (14.8)	6 (5.7)	Pronunciation, Methods of Teaching, Development of Model questions.	5 days	SCERT	Nil

Note: Figures within ( ) represent percentages.

5.17.5 Programme Specific Capacity Building Courses

SCERT and the Orissa Primary Education Programme Authority (OPEPA) organized a few courses as part of their programmes. These courses are programme specific. The extent to which DIET and STS faculty participated in these programmes is reflected in Table 5.18.

In five areas of concern such as, Non-formal Education, Population Education, ECCE, Action Research and local games and songs for context specific classroom process, SCERT and OPEPA organized courses for TEs. TEs would, in turn, train primary school teachers in these programme specific areas.

The following facts are evident from the Table 5.18:

- The courses being programme specific, selected TEs were given training for effective implementation of programmes through DIETs and STSs. Precisely, these TEs acted as Programme-in-charge in DIETs and STSs. Non-formal Education was a GOI sponsored programme intended to reach out the drop-outs and the never-enrolled.
- DIETs and STSs were assigned with the task of effective implementation of the programmes. One-third of TEs of DIETs and nearly one-quarter (23.6%) of TEs of STSs participated in the courses on NFE. The proportion could be 100 per cent if the number of Resource Persons selected for the Non-formal programme would have been known. To put it simply, almost all selected RPs of DIETs and STSs should have been trained.
- Population Education was a GOI sponsored and UNFPA funded Project. Twenty-four TEs out of 135 have been trained. Probably, the project intended to have a small group of competent and committed TEs to oversee the effective implementation of this project. In this, it would be a gross underestimation of TEs who were really meant for the project. Extent of participation (17.7%) is, therefore, apparent, not real.

TABLE 5.18

Participation of TEs in Programme Specific Training Courses

Sl. No.	*Name of the Courses*	*No. and % of Teacher Educators attended*		*Content*	*Duration*	*Organized by*	*Any follow-up*
		DDIETs No.	*STSs No.*				
1.	Non-formal Educatiion	45 (33.0)	25(23.6)	Importance of NFE teaching Lang, Math, Eng, Scie.	10 days	SCERT	Nil
2.	Population Education	24 (17.7)	Nil	Content analysis From classes (I to VII)	5 days	SCERT	Nil
3.	Early Childhood Education and Care (ECCE)	26 (19.3)	Nil	All the subject areas and practical.	10 days	SCERT	Nil
4.	Action Research	30 (22.2)	Nil	How to write Research report	5 days	SCERT & DPEP	Nil
5.	Local games 26 (19.3) and Songs	Nil		Collection of local Songs and games	3 days	SCERT	Nil

Note: Figures within ( ) represent percentages.

- Similarly, ECCE was implemented as a component of DPEP interventions, for which a select set of TEs was entrusted with the task. Although the apparent percentage of participation was as low as 19.3, the real extent of participation could be somewhere near 100 per cent as training for Project Personnel was a mandatory requirement.
- Action Research Projects were undertaken by some interested and academic-oriented TEs. The course was for these TEs whose research proposals were selected by an Expert Committee for financial support from DPEP. Therefore, the courses were mandatory for those TEs. In that sense, all 30 TEs, representing cent percent, participated in the course. The apparent figure of 22.2 per cent is, therefore, to be taken with caveat.
- SCERT compiled local songs and games, mostly from tribal areas, that could be used to teach school subjects. In other words, though primary school curriculum was developed at the state level, its effective transaction could be carried out locally using those local specific songs and games. The 26 TEs, identified from tribal DIETs, were given training by SCERT.
- Non-involvement of TEs of STSs could possibly be due to their low "visibility" as Teacher Education Institutions, partly due to being eclipsed by DIETs, and partly to their preoccupation with training, hardly going beyond the trodden track.

5.18 TEACHER EDUCATORS ATTITUDE TOWARDS INTERNAL VARIABLES

Research in India and around the world has shown that both home and school investments are important in enhancing students' learning. Some home and school inputs are more effective than others. Some are, more cost-effective, others aren't. . . , Teachers' satisfaction with the amount s/he gets, cordial relationship with colleague, enabling facilities for research, availability of funds and relationships with and care for children are important variables that impact an institution's performance. Teachers' own perception about these variables are significant predictors. Table 5.19 presents TEs' attitude towards these interval variables.

A close look at the figures presented in the Table 5.19 makes the following evident:

- Salaries and other associated benefits are important factors that motivate individuals in any profession. Nearly, 52 per cent of TEs of DIETs viewed their salaries as fair and poor. On the other extreme, only less than two per cent of TEs felt that their salaries were excellent. On the other hand, 67 per cent of TEs of STSs felt that their salaries were somehow manageable (fair + poor). This perception of TEs about their salaries tends to affect their performance. If salaries are perceived to be too low, teacher absenteeism is likely to be high because teachers must supplement their earnings with other jobs. Low perceived salaries work as a major disincentive for good performance.
- In TEIs, it is the relationship that matters. Working as a team, with a strong bond of relationships, enhances both individual and institutional effectiveness and productivity. Relationship rated "excellent" by TEs in DIETs and STSs is a bare 15 per cent and 18 per cent respectively. While 52 per cent of TEs of DIETs viewed their colleagial relationship good, the corresponding figure of TEs in STSs is found to be higher by 10 percentage points (62.3%). Probably, relatively small staff size and the homogeneity of STSs contribute to institutional cohesiveness. Conversely, large staff size and divergent background of TEs and other supporting staff tended to create dissensions among staff members of DIETs.
- Research is a major activity in TEIs, more particularly in DIETs. Despite this, about 17 per

TABLE 5.19

Teacher Educators' Attitude Towards Internal Variables

Rating	*Towards Salary*		*Relation between teaching & Non-teaching*		*Research Facility*		*Availability of funds*		*Relation with students*	
	DIET Nos.	*STS Nos.*	*DIET Nos.*	*STS Nos.*	*DIET Nos.*	*STS Nos.*	*DIET Nos.*	*STS Nos.*	*DIET Nos.*	*STS Nos.*
Excelent	2(1.5)	2(1.9)	20(14.8)	19(17.9)	2(1.5)	-	-	-	40(29.6)	34(32.1)
Good	63(46.7)	33(31.1)	70(51.9)	66(62.3)	33(24.4)	21(19.9)	15(11.1)	18(17.0)	78(57.8)	57(53.8)
Fair	47(34.8)	51(48.1)	40(29.6)	17(16.9)	37(27.4)	23(17.7)	19(14.1)	24(22.7)	17(12.6)	15(14.1)
Poor	23(17.0)	20(18.9)	5 (03.7)	4 (03.8)	64(46.7)	62(58.5)	71(52.6)	64(60.3)	-	-
Total	135(100)	106(100)	135(100)	106(100)	135(100)	106(100)	135(100)	106(1000)	135(100)	106(100)

Note: Figures within ( ) represent percentages.

cent of TEs rated the facilities in DIETs for research as "poor." Probably non-provision of funds for research and non-release of research grants contributed to such an impression.

As expected, on the other hand, STSs didn't have none of the facilities for research: neither a good library, nor funds, and nor even research-oriented leadership.

- One of the disturbing features is that nearly 53 TEs of DIETs and 60.3 per cent of TEs in STSs rated the availability of funds as "poor." This is true in respect of Non-plan for which funds are scarce on account of severe fiscal crunch of the State Government. DIETs have, on the other hand, funds but not released by GOI in time or not released by the State Government at all. Thus, DIETs live amidst a paradox-poverty of funds, amidst plenty. Huge GOI funds remain unutilised.
- On the other extreme of the scale, not even a single TE of DIETs considered availability of funds "excellent," notwithstanding substantial support from Government of India.
- A silver lining that is visibly pronounced is teacher-student relationship. About 30.0 per cent of TEs of DIETs and nearly one-third of TEs of STSs rated the relationship as "excellent." An appreciably large segment of TEs said that relationship with students was 'good': the percentages of TEs in DIETs and STSs are being 58.00 and 54 percent respectively.

Tables 5.20, 5.21, 5.22, 5.23, and 5.24 reflect the outcomes Chi-square test.

5.19 MEMBERSHIP OF TEs IN PROFESSIONAL ASSOCIATIONS

One of the means of rejuvenating professionalism among TEs involves the formation of unions or professional associations. Professionalism is assiduously acquired, it is

TABLE 5.20

Contingency Table for Chi-square Test of Independence between the Attitude of Teacher Educators towards Salary and the Type of Institutions

Category	*DIETs*	*STSs*	*Total*
Excellent	2 (2.24)	2 (1.76)	4
Good	63 (53.78)	33 (42.22)	96
Fair	47 (54.90)	51 (43.10)	98
Poor	23 (24.09)	20 (18.91)	43
Total	135	106	241

Note: Figures within ( ) represent percentages.
X^2 = 6.361 df = 3, Not Significant at 0.05 level.

TABLE 5.21

Contingency Table for Chi-square Test of Independence between the Attitude of Teacher Educators towards the Relationship between Teaching and Non-Teaching and the Type of Institutions

Category	*DIETs*	*STSs*	*Total*
Excellent	20 (21.85)	19 (17.15)	39
Good	70 (76.18)	66 (59.82)	136
Fair	40 (31.93)	17 (25.07	57
Poor	5 (5.04)	4 (3.96)	9
Total	135	106	241

Note: Figures within ( ) represent percentages.
X^2 = 6.041 df = 3, Not Significant at 0.05 level.

TABLE 5.22

Contingency Table for Chi-square Test of Independence between the Attitude of Teacher Educators towards the Availability of Research Facility and the Type of Institutions

Category	*DIETs*	*STSs*	*Total*
Excellent	2 (1.12)	0 (.88)	2
Good	33 (30.25)	21 (23.75)	54
Fair	37 (33.61)	23 (26.39)	60
Poor	63 (70.02)	62 (54.48)	125
Total	135	106	241

Note: Figures within ( ) represent percentages.
X^2 = 3.652 df = 3. Not Significant at 0.05 level.

TABLE 5.23

Contingency Table for Chi-square Test of Independence between the Attitude of Teacher Educators towards the Availlability of Funds from Different Sources and Type of Institutions

Category	*DIETs*	*STSs*	*Total*
Excellent	0 (0)	0 (0)	0
Good	15 (16.42))	18 (16.58)	33
Fair	19 (21.46)	24 (21.60)	43
Poor	71 (67.18)	64 (67.82)	135
Total	105	106	211

Note: Figures within ( ) represent percentages.
X^2 = 1.213 df = 3. Not Significant at 0.05 level

TABLE 5.24

Contingency Table for Chi-square Test of Independence between the Attitude of Teacher Educators towards the Relation with the Student and Type of Institutions

Category	*DIETs*	*STSs*	*Total*
Excellent	40 (41.45)	34 (32.55)	74
Good	78 (75.62)	57 (59.38)	135
Fair	17 (17.93)	15 (14.07)	32
Poor	0	0	0
Total	135	106	241

Note: Figures within ( ) represent percentages.
X^2 = 0.395 df = 3. Not Significant at 0.05 level.

never ascribed. It is found that a limited number of TEs of DIETs had enrolled themselves as members in different professional associations such as, Indian Association of Educational Planning and Administration, Sishu Vikas Kendra, Rotary Club, Indian Association of Teacher Educators, Indian Association of Pre-school Education, Bharat Gyan Vigyan Samiti, All India People's Science Network, Society for Learning, Research and Development, Zilla Saksharta Samiti, Sishu Sahitya Academy, Physically Handicapped Association, etc. Contrary to this, only four Teacher Educators of STSs were members of the Board of Secondary Education, Orissa, Aurobindo Education Centre, and Orissa Government Teachers' Association.

Professional Associations are expected to perform two major tasks: first, to protect the professional interests and rights of their members; and second, to enhance their professional competencies and capacities. Not offen one they are preoccupied with the former task, hardly doing justice to the latter. Mere membership in professional associations speaks nothing about the extent and quality of participation, leading to professional development. Therefore, quality of participation is of prime importance.

5.20 VISIT TO FOREIGN COUNTRIES

Visit to foreign countries for academic purpose is almost absent in DIETs. Only one TE from one of the DIETs visited UK on a British Council Fellowship on Non-formal Education, that too in 1980s. Non-Participation of TEs in exposure visits to institutions abroad is essentially due to non-existence of provision for such programmes. In India fellowships for higher studies in the developed countries are the exclusive preserve of Higher Education.

5.21 RESEARCH STUDIES

Research is one of the grey areas in TEIs, particularly in DIETs let alone in STSs. Despite the intended objective of fostering a climate for undertaking research studies and getting them published, research is yet to take a firm root in DIETs. Only 12 TEs out of 135 in DIETs undertook research studies and still less got their studies published. Only three TEs published their books on Education and Oriya literature. They are, however, not based on researches. This low scale research activity speaks of the gross deficit of academic interest on the part of TEs and lack of institutional leadership. One of the persistently pervasive perceptions that has led to such a bleak scenario is that conducting research is perceived to be the exclusive preserve of institutions of higher learning. This myth still pervades the psyche of the DIET faculty. In spite of funds being available from DPEP/SSA for undertaking research studies the position continues to be discouraging.

5.22 EXPERTS' VIEWS ON ELEMENTARY TEACHER EDUCATION PROGRAMME

It was felt imperative to capture the views and vision of experts in the field of Elementary Teacher Education. For this, an opinionnaire was designed by the researcher. The wavelength of the instrument covered some critical areas of concern: (i) duality in the structure of Elementary Teacher Education in the State, (ii) entry qualification of candidates

TABLE 5.25

Views and Visions of Experts on Elementary Teacher Education Programme

Sl. No.	*Broad areas Concern*		*Sub-areas Visions*	*Views and of Concern*	*Percentage of of experts.*
1	*2*		*3*	*4*	*5*
1.0	Structure of Elementary Teachers. Education Institutions	1.1	Type of ETEIs	• A single type TEIs, i.e. DIETs and STSs,with identical staff infrastructure and functions	80.0
		1.2	DIETs Advantage	• DIETs are better placed in terms of staff, infrastructure and research	90.0
		1.3	Academic climate and institutional quality	• DIETs have been conceived as "Centres of Excellence" and pace-selling institutions in Teacher Education	100.0
				• Notwithstanding this, almost all DIETs function at the sub-optional level, i.e. enough space for effective and efficient functioning	95.0
		1.3	Branches and their functionality	•Roles and functions of seven Branches not clearly defined	70.0
				• TEIs placed in various Branches don't have required competence and skills	90.0

(Contd.)

TABLE 5.25 (CONTD.)

1	2	3	4	5
			• SCERT to envision the role perception of different Branches	96.0
			• Capacity of DIET faculty in the specific	100.0
			• Branch needs to be developed Branch specific performance needs to be objectively assessed and accountability be fixed	100.0
		1.4 Making STSs comparable to DIETs: comparable inputs, and outputs.	• All STSs be upgraded to DIETs	25.0
			• 30 districts to have 30 DIETs in the way of an ST Schools upgraded.	75.0
		1.5 Duration of the course and the curriculum	• The duration of the two-year Certificate Course is adequate. However, time-on-task needs to be optimized	80.0
			• In view of the duration of the Course and entry qualification (twelve years of schooling), the Course be upgraded from a Certificate Course to a Diploma Course	78.0
			• The curriculum needs to be renewed at	100.0

			least once in every five years to make it more relevant, need-based and context specific. Moreover, it should follow reformulation of elementary school curriculum.	
2..0	Making DIETs functional	2.1 Putting faculty in position and promotion on the basis of performance	• Large number of posts lying vacant	100.0
			• Adequately and appropriately qualified faculty be recruited through systematic and stringent procedure	100.0
			• Rationalization in placement of existing faculty to ensure their availability in all DIETs	96.0
			• Need for lateral entry of teachers with prescribed qualification. preferably from Elementary Cadre, as per Personnel Policy (1990) as Faculty in DIETs	75.0
			• Indiscriminate placement of teachers of Secondary schools as faculty in DIETs, without prescribed qualification be done away with	80.0
			The present practice of placing Class I Officers of Secondary Cadre as Principals needs to be stopped and they are to be selected through a stringent selection process.	77.0

(Contd.)

TABLE 5.25 (CONTD.)

1	2	3	4	5
			Ideally the posts of Principals be filled up by way of promotion of STEs of DIETs	
			• The seven Branches can be made functional only when adequately qualified and competent faculty are recruited and placed in	85.0
			• A fixed percentage of posts of STEs be filled up through promotion strictly on the basis of performance of TEs in teaching, research, publication and innovations	
3..0	Staff Development	3.1 Capacity building of faculty	• In-service training of TEs at regular intervals to update and upgrade their knowledge, skills and competencies be systematically planned and organized, in particular using appropriate communication technologies	100.0
			• Distance Education mode may be used to train all TEs put in place	66.0
			• Induction level training, which is almost non-existent, be made mandatory	98.0
			• Teacher Educators be tested to assess their value addition due to their participation in in in-service training programmes	75.0
			• Given the importance of research into the qualitative improvement of teaching, Teacher	80.0

				Education (both pre-service and in-service) should include a stronger component of training for research	
				• Participation in refresher courses for professional development be made mandatory for TEs, and this be considered as a criterion for promotion	76.0
4..0	Evaluating Trainees' performance			• Evaluating performance to be a right mix of internal and external evaluation: ideal ratio being: 60% and 40%	23.0
				• Trainees' performance be evaluated only by those who teach in ETEIs, not by Secondary School Teachers who are not conversant with Elementary Teacher Education Programme	77.0
				• Teaching being on profession, Teacher Education Programme needs to develop a repertoire of skills, and attitudes, which must receive overriding priority	90.0
5.0	Academic rigor of the Teacher Education Programme	5.1	Qualification of Teacher Educators	• Adoption of GOI and NCTE stipulated qualifications, such as a Master's Degree in a school subject with a Master's Degree in Pedagogy (M.Ed) to be strictly adhered to	83.0
				• TEs must be acquainted with the contextual mandates that affect the ways young children learn	80.0

(Contd.)

TABLE 5.25 (CONTD.)

1	2	3	4	5
			• Action research, i.e., research by practicing TEs, should inform one's teaching and pedagogical strategies and practices Instrumentality of Action Research is to be realized by TEs	85.0
			• Teacher Educators, in collaboration with Student-teachers, to prepare Teaching Learning Materials	77.0
			• Teacher Education Institutions should not work in isolation. Synergic linkages to be forged with ICDS, school supervision machinery, VECs, SC and ST Development Department, etc	72.0
			• NCTE, a statutory body, created by an Act of Parliament of India, is to move away from its rigid preoccupation with physical norms and standards, and take positive steps towards ensuring quality and excellence in Teacher Education	76.0
			• Teacher Educators' Association, covering DIETs and Elementary Teacher Education Institutions, at the national and state level should be formed for development of professionalism and professional excellence	85.0

who seek admission to ETEIs, (iii) curriculum structure, (iv) academic pursuits of faculty in DIETs and ST Schools in terms of undertaking research studies, (v) educational and professional preparation of Teacher Educators, (vi) the system of evaluation in ETEIs, and (vii) the patterns and directions of change of the system keeping in view the contours of emerging development.

The views and visions of the experts, collected through the opinionnaire, have been presented in the Table 5.25.

To sum up the discussion attempted in this subsection, the following overall observations appeared to be appropriate:

(i) Two sets of Elementary Teacher Education Institutions viz. Secondary Training Schools, and District Institute of Education and Training were distinctly marked by unacceptable disparities, which tended to create inequity in provision of education and training.

(ii) A sizeable number of experts expressed their dissatisfaction and discontent with the functioning of DIETs, conceived in the mould of centers of excellence and pace-setting institutions, which functioned at the sub-optimal level. Perceived institutional "vision" was largely belied. Result: more rhetorics, little reality; more light, little heat; and a lot of sound without substance.

(iii) Suggestions of experts, based on their own assessment of the state of art as well as their vision, provided the patterns and directions of reform and policy options.

5.23 HIGHLIGHTS OF PARTICIPANT OBSERVATION

As mentioned in the Methodology Chapter (Chapter IV), the researcher endeavoured to have an in-depth and involved observation of the 'processes' of functioning of ETEIs. The precise purpose of developing an Observation Schedule was to capture the quality of "processes", which very often gets lost on account of overriding emphasis on outcomes.

The researcher herself visited 24 STSs and 11 DIETs constituting 44.4 and 84.4 per cent of ETEIs respectively. Besides observing the "processes", the researcher had interaction with the Principals/Headmasters and the faculty of the institutions. The following are some of the notable observations:

- Secondary Training Schools were, by and large, confronted with the problem of acute shortage of teaching staff. Ironically, as against a standard faculty of NCTE, STSs did not have a uniform staff structure. Creation of posts varied from institution to institution despite the fact that all STSs offered the same two-year pre-service course with a uniform intake per year. The situation is inexplicable.
- Creation of posts apart, staff in position in different STSs varied widely. For instance, whereas 40.7 per cent STSs were fully staffed, 24.1 per cent STSs had 80 to 100 per cent posts filled up, and 11.1 per cent STSs had less than 40 per cent faculty in position. This created two kinds of problems: first, many classes had unscheduled suspension on almost no time-on task as they were being taken by an already over-stretched teacher. As observed, no meaningful instruction took place, leading to wastage of instructional hours.
- Almost 50.0 per cent of faculty did not possess NCTE on GOI stipulated qualifications, i.e. MA/ MSc./MEd. These teachers, as classroom observations indicated, fell deplorably short of the expected level of performance. Moreover, with paradigm shift in classroom transaction, focusing on activity based and constructivist pedagogy, these TEs were found to be nowhere rear even the minimal level of performance. The situation led inexorably to sub-standard classroom processes. Despite NCTE's rigid stance on conforming with its norms and standards, no policy is yet in place to put faculty with requisite qualification in STSs.

- One-third of STSs did not have Headmasters. Out of the existing Headmasters, almost 70.0 per cent did not have stipulated qualifications. Rarely did the Headmasters teach, let alone teaching effectively. Classes of TEs were never supervised by the Headmasters. Nor did the Headmasters reviewed the performance of their colleagues. This reflects the quality of instructional leadership the Headmasters offered.
- As evident from the records it was found that the courses slanted as late as September for a couple of years due to inordinate delay in admission. This practice starkly contrasted with the NCTE norms as well as the laid down policy of the state Government about the commencement of academic session from July. This amounted to substantial reduction in the prescribed number of teaching days. To put it differently, the quality of instruction suffered a setback.
- Compared to STSs, DIETs seemed to have a standardized faculty structure common to all Indian States. This is primarily on account of GOI Guidelines (1989). However, the State Government had separate designation in place of Lecturers and Senior Lecturer to avoid confusion with similar posts in institutions of higher education under the Department of Higher Education. In a DIET, the standard staff structure consists of a Principal, a Vice-Principal, six Senior Teacher Educators and 14 Teacher Educators. In contrary to this, two DIETs: DIET, Ganjam at Kholikote and DIET Balasore at Remuna had a slim staff structure viz. a Principal, two Senior Teacher Educators and eight posts of Teacher Educator. This shows that creation of posts in these two DIETs and DIETs sanctioned later was exclusively dictated by the policy for structural adjustment disregard of academic and quality considerations. Paradoxically, Ganjam and Balasore are the two districts which have larger number of elementary

schools and teachers, hence larger demand for in-service training. A closer insight into the system revealed that it is the Finance Department, not the Education Department that matters.

- A disturbing phenomenon, evidently visible, in two sets of DIETs was concentration of faculty in DIETs located nearer to State Capital or Cuttack, the commercial capital of Orissa and skeleton faculty in DIETs of other distinctly, more particularly in DIETs of KBK (Koraput, Kalahandi and Balangir) districts. This accentuates the disadvantages and disparities these socio-economically and educationally backward districts have been historically inflicted by. Nothing has been done to redress the plight of the DIETs of these districts, despite State Government's commitment to development of these districts. In other words, the State Government found it difficult to stick to its placement policy by the sheer force of power the politicians, bureaucrats and elites wielded.
- Composition of faculty represented a mix of people with diverse background: some directly recruited by the State Selection Board, fresh and inexperienced; some through lateral entry from secondary education cadre largely not conversant with Teacher Education course; and some from defunct B.Ed. Colleges, with an attitude of big brother and superiority complex. It was evident from close observation that the faculty largely lacked cohesiveness to work as an academic team, and a simmering sense of dissension was robustly visible. This, to a large extent, affected the institutional climate. Vision building and striving towards transforming the vision into a reality were therefore, threatened and frustrated. This 'relationship' was found to have sapped the institutional improvement initiatives.
- Almost all DIETs visited did not have a Principal with a vision and a mission. The 'image' of a

Principal, based on observational evidence, was that of a superior authority, with a command and control mindset, not that of a facilitator, a motivator, a team coordinator, leader of pedagogy and a collegial sharing co-worker. The absence of an enabling mindset affected the morale and performance of the faculty.

- Innovations and positive practices are considered the 'life-blood' of DIETs. DIETs activities have, by and large, remained confined to conducting pre-service and in-service courses. This is largely due to a heterogeneous faculty-mix and lack of leadership at the institutional level. Wherever innovations have been tried out, it is due to individually endeavour, not to institutional initiative.
- Despite acute shortage of TEs, poor infrastructural facilities, and inadequately qualified faculty in STSs, the results of the STSs in the final Examinations conducted by the Board of Secondary Education were comparable or even sometimes better than that of the DIETs. This could be explained partly by the liberal assessment by the examiners and partly by evaluation by secondary school teachers who are hardly conversant with the content of the Teacher Education course.

When asked to point out the problems the STSs are experiencing, the TEs of STSs observed that:

- acute shortage of faculty, particularly in STSs located in KBK districts, affected their normal instructional programmes;
- dearth or inadequacy, of hostel accommodation was a major deficit;
- introduction of Project work as a part of the preservice Teachers education curriculum in the absence of required number of TEs made them overworked and put the student teachers in difficulty;

- STSs are hardly supervised by the higher authorities. None do the Headmasters supervise the classes of TEs, which has baneful effects on their performance;
- there existed no staff development programme for the Headmasters of STSs to work with efficiency and effectiveness as leaders of co-functional teams; and
- TEs of STSs did not have the opportunity of participating in capacity building programme for their professional development;

Similarly, DIETs, also faced a few problems. These included:

- The absence of a clearly defined cadre for DIET faculty, despite the mandates of the Personnel Policy (1989), jeopardizes the professional interests of the faculty. This aside, the non-creation of the cadre works as a demotivating factor for better faculty performance.
- Non-posting of suitable qualified Principals created a void, leading to poor or no instructional leadership in DIETs.
- Inordinate delay in selection of candidates for admission to CT course led to loss of precious instructional days. This could largely be attributed to the centralized selection by SCERT. DIETs could have been delegated this responsibility. Decentralization could possibly create a climate of faith and freedom in DIETs.
- DIETs have not been involved in the State and National level capacity building prgorammes by OPEPA, SCERT, NCERT and NIEPA as institutions. On the other hand a handful of selected, nevertheless competent and committed, TEs have been involved. The involvement of DIETs as institutions, in such programmes needs to be broad-based.

In short, for a number of reasons, notwithstanding clearly stipulated guidelines, DIETs have yet to develop into robust and vibrant institutions for nurturance of excellence and quality. This will, in turn, affect the quality of the Elementary Education system of the State. Teacher Education continues to have "low visibility" in the education system on account of non-appreciation of its potential. What is pressingly urgent is a change in the perspective of decision-makers and policy-framers. Particularly at the state level, towards Teacher Education sub-system.

5.24 IN-SERVICE TRAINING COURSES FOR TEACHERS' CAPACITY BUILDING

Teachers are central to the delivery as well as the quality of education. Teacher training institutions, force the daunting challenge of preparing training and retraining vast numbers of primary teachers. Teachers' effectiveness is largely determined by: first their general academic preparation; second, quality of pre-service training teachers have undergone; and third, the quality and relevance of in-service training courses. In-service capacity building courses for, practicing teachers compensate their initial entry deficits and equip them with new pedagogical skills and competencies. In-service training courses for practicing teachers are primarily based on the practices that enhance student learning, such as: (i) require students to participate actively, (ii) allow students to practice what is being taught and apply it to their own experience, (iii) monitor and evaluate student performance, and (iv) give students appropriate feedback on their performance.

With this perspective, TEIs, mostly DIETs, conducted a series of in-service courses, for practicing primary teachers. The impact these courses have depends, among other things, on the need and relevance, adequacy and coverage duration, venues, method of delivery, evaluation and feedback and monitoring of the courses. The researcher endeavoured to assess the breadth and depth of these courses through a structured Interview schedule. She interviewed 24 assistant teachers of STSs and 30 TEs of DIETs on various aspects of in-service training courses.

Some of the notable views that emerged from the interviews included:

- The wavelength of in-service courses included primarily three types of courses viz. content enrichment, activity-based interactive pedagogy programme specific courses like Population Education, Environment Education, etc.
- Emerging areas of interventions such as field interaction, community participation, Village Education Committees, Parents Teachers' Associations as grassroots level structures were required to be covered.
- The Resource Persons were drawn from internal and external sources. However, internal Resource Persons constituted the mainstay of the resource support system. It emerged from the interviews that the involvement of external resource persons on a larger scale could possibly improve the quality of such programmes.
- For increased participation of teachers in in-service training courses, venues be nearer to the place of work of teachers.
- It was observed, almost without exception, that extent of transmission loss from one level to the other was high. The value addition could be made more sustainable if the course delivery mechanism is made more participatory. Real import of training skills, required through such courses, to classroom could be made widespread and extensive if the contents and delivery strategies are tailored to the contextual realities.
- It was also felt that such courses needed to take advantage of the revolutionary developments in the field of Information and Communication Technology.

5.25 SUMMING UP

The analysis of data, collected through a variety of

instruments, brought to focus the state of Elementary Teacher Education Programme in the state. More particularly, it revealed the strengths and weaknesses of the system, possibilities for its reform and renewal in response to emerging developments, systemic inertia and reluctance to change, needed policy options, and insights to make the system work informed by "visions and voices" of stakeholders. In brief, a change in mind-set, of policy and decision-makers and political masters and teachers and Teacher Educators, the critical actors, should precede systemic changes. Conclusions and recommendations in the next chapter are largely based on the findings of this chapter.

6

Conclusions

A. SUMMARY

6.1 INTRODUCTION

India's destiny is being shaped in her classrooms. In this age of Science and Technology, education seeks to give happiness and security to the people. The chief aims of national reconstruction is to raise the standard of living, which depends upon the merit and number of our school and college students. Children are our future and investment in our children holds the key to the future development of the country. No capital is as valuable as human capital.

As envisaged in the National Policy on Education, 1986 (with modifications in 1992, p. 03), "Life in the coming decades is likely to bring new tensions together with unprecedented opportunities. To enable the people to benefit in the new environment, it will require new design of human resource development. The coming generation should have the ability to internalise new ideas constantly and creatively. They have to be imbued with a strong commitment to human values and social justice. All these imply better education." Therefore, the concept of national system of education implies that up to a given level all students, irrespective of caste, creed, location or sex, have access to education of a comparable quality. But the above objective can only be materialised through training and imparting relevant knowledge and life skills in our regular classroom transaction process.

It is universally accepted that the quality of education significantly depends on the quality of teachers. In the words of the University Education Commission (1948), "The success of educational process depends much on the character and ability of the Teacher." No teacher who is not a master of the field, who is not in touch with the latest development in his subject and untrammeled mind will ever succeed in inspiring youth. So the right kind of teacher is he who possesses a vivid awareness of his mission. He not only loves his subject, he loves also those whom he teaches."

"Teacher Education" refers to the structure; institutions and processes by means of which men and women are prepared for work in elementary and secondary schools.

According to the Encyclopedic Dictionary of Education, Teacher Education is the very broad field of study and instruction concerned with professional preparation for careers in teaching, administration or other specialisation in education, particularly at the levels of pre-school, elementary and secondary education. It is also called professional teacher education.

According to Good's Dictionary of Education (1959, p. 550), "Teacher Education means all the formal and informal activities and experiences that help to qualify a person to assume the responsibilities of a member of the educational profession or to discharge his responsibilities more effectively."

International Encyclopedia of Teaching and Teacher Education says (1987, p. 77), "Teacher Education or teacher development can be considered in three phases: pre-service, induction and in-service. The three phases are considered as parts of a continuous process."

The NCTE (1998, p. 23) observes that Teacher Education Programmes shall focus on competencies and commitment. Since the teacher has responsibility for the total development of the child and to prepare him or her as a citizen having faith in and professing democratic, secular and socialistic values, his own education and training should lead to the inculcation of similar values and skills based on appropriate learning experiences.

The structural changes in institutional infrastructure have been brought about and DIETs have been established as per the guidelines of MHRD (1989) to provide academic and resource support at the grass root level for the success of various strategies and programmes being undertaken in the area of elementary education.

At present, there are 13 (thirteen) DIETs and 55 ST Schools in Orissa. As per the approved staffing pattern, there were 544 Teacher Educators working in both the institutions (DIETs and STSs). With a view to knowing the comparative status of the Teacher Educators, their academic and professional growth, the investigator proposed to conduct the study entitled "AN ACADEMIC AND PROFESSIONAL PROFILE OF TEACHER EDUCATORS AT THE ELEMENTARY EDUCATION LEVEL", so that suitable action plan can be developed for improving the existing condition.

6.2 OBJECTIVES OF THE STUDY

(i) To collect demographic data about Teacher Educators of Orissa.

(ii) To know their academic background.

(iii) To ascertain their professional growth.

(iv) To compare their role preference *versus* role performance of Teacher Educators working in ST Schools and DIETs.

(v) To develop professional and academic profile of Teacher Educators for initiating plan of action for improvement of academic and professional growth of Teacher Educators working in ST Schools and DIETs.

6.3 SCOPE OF THE STUDY

The scope of the study include:

(a) Confined to all the Teacher Educators of 13 DIETs and 52 ST Schools of Orissa.

(b) Confined to all three major aspects of the teachers' profile, i.e. (i) Demographic Variables, (ii) Academic Variables, and (iii) Professional Variables.
(c) Confined to the period ending with the year 1998.

There were other important dimensions like social commitment of Teacher Educators, their psychological and political considerations that were deliberately excluded in present study.

6.4 METHOD OF STUDY

The present study adopted the descriptive-cum-survey method and followed the allied approaches for its various dimensions.

6.5 SAMPLE OF THE STUDY

In the present study, however, sampling was not done. So all the DIETs and ST Schools and all the full-time Teacher Educators of DIETs and ST Schools of Orissa brought under the purview of the study.

The total number of Teacher Educators present in 13 DIETs and 52 ST Schools of Orissa was 544 in the year 1998.

6.6 RESEARCH TOOLS

The tools used in the present study were:

(i) A questionnaire for the Teacher-Educators named as **"Teacher Educator Data Form"**
(ii) An Opinionnaire for experts
(iii) An Observation Schedule to collect data about the institutions
(iv) An Interview Schedule for Teacher Educators

6.7 PROCEDURE OF DATA COLLECTION

The lists of Teacher Educators of different DIETs and ST

Schools were collected from the SCERT (Orissa), Bhubaneswar. Then, the data were collected from the Teacher Educators of DIETs and ST Schools with the help of the questionnaire mainly through personal contact and also by mail.

The personnel associated with Elementary Teacher Education Programme were individually interviewed through the structured Opinionnaire.

With the help of an Observation Schedule, the investigator collected data about DIETs and ST Schools from the records and documents of the Institutions.

The investigator used an Interview Schedule to collect data from the Teacher Educators about the in-service Training Programmes conducted in the institutions.

6.8. ANALYSIS OF DATA

The collected data were compiled, tabulated and analysed using various statistical calculations like percentage, means, T-test, etc. Interpretation was done accordingly.

6.9. MAJOR FINDINGS

6.9.1 Questionnaire

The major findings of the study were grouped under:

(i) Demographic,
(ii) Academic,
(iii) Professional.

(i) Demographic

- The number of DIETs and ST Schools in Orissa was 13 and 52 respectively. The total numbers of Teacher Educators were 544.
- The entire population of teacher education institutions and Teacher Educators were brought under the purview of the study.
- The highest percentages of Teacher Educators were in the age group of 40-44 years and 45-49 years in the DIETs and ST Schools respectively.

- Besides 18 percentage of Teacher Educators of both DIETs and ST Schools would reach the retirement age during next five years.
- In the DIETs, male Teacher Educators constituted 67 percentages and female Teacher Educators 33 percentage, while in ST Schools the male and female counterparts constituted 79 percentages and 21 percentages respectively.
- In the ST Schools, 100 percentage of Teacher Educators were Hindus but in DIETs about 3 percentages of Teacher Educators were Christians and Mohammedan and 97 percentages of Teacher Educators were Hindus.
- As regards the caste, the highest percentage, i.e. (28.7) Teacher Educators of DIETs and 22.6 percentage of Teacher Educators of ST Schools belonged to OBC and only four and eight per cent belonged to SC and ST category.
- About 73 percentage of the Teacher Educators of DIETs and 79 percentages of Teacher Educators of ST Schools represented the rural population whereas 27 percentages and 21 percentages of Teacher Educators of DIETs and ST Schools respectively were urban representation.
- The majority of the Teacher Educators of DIETs and ST Schools (i.e. 55.5% and 56.6% respectively) possessed average health.
- Majority of Teacher Educators working in DIETs and ST Schools (i.e. 79% and 80% respectively) were married. Remaining 21 percentage and 15 percentage were unmarried. Almost very negligible percentage of Teacher Educators were separated.
- As high as 46 percentage of Teacher Educators of DIETs and 33 percentage of Teacher Educators of ST Schools had only one or two children, whereas 25 percentage of Teacher Educators in both the cases had no children. Only 1% and 2% respectively in case of DIETs and ST Schools had seven or more than seven children.

(ii) Academic

- Respectively 6% and 13% of Teacher Educators of DIETs possessed Ph.D. and M.Phil. Degree but in case of ST Schools none of them possessed Ph.D. or M.Phil. Degree. Likewise, 12% and 58% of Teacher Educators of DIETs possessed M.Sc and M.A. Degree respectively. In case of ST Schools, the percentages of Teacher Educators with M.Sc and M.A. qualification were 3% and 25% respectively. 22% in case of DIETs and 35% in case of ST Schools possessed B.A. Degree. 8% and 17% respectively in case of DIETs and ST Schools possessed B.Sc. Degree.
- As regards the professional qualification, 47 percentage of Teacher Educators of DIETs and 23 percentage of Teacher Educators of ST Schools possessed M.Ed Degree.
- Instead of professional degrees like M.Ed./B.Ed., 15 per cent and 20 percentage in case of DIETs and ST Schools respectively possessed other degrees like Diploma in Sahityacharya, Ratna, B.P.Ed., PGDHE (IGNOU), Fine Arts, C.P.Ed. They represent subsidiary academic staff such as Hindi/ Sanskrit Teachers, Physical Education Teacher, Art Education Instructor, etc.
- 10 percentage of Teacher Educators of DIETs were conducting research for the Ph.D. Degree.
- About the relative role preference, the calculated value found to be significant at 0.01 level of confidence. Hence, the relative role preference of Teacher Educators serving in DIETs differs from that of the Teacher Educators serving in ST Schools.
- As high as 33 percentage of Teacher Educators, both in case of DIETs and ST Schools were interested both in teaching and research but leaning towards teaching.
- The percentage of research preference of Teacher Educators of DIETs was higher than that of ST

Schools. (i.e. in DIETs 06% and in ST Schools 02%).

- 17 percentage of Teacher Educators of DIETs and 8 percentage Teacher Educators of ST Schools had publications to their credit.
- As regards the articles published numbering (1-5), the percentage of Teacher Educators in DIETs was 12 and in ST Schools 6.
- The Teacher Educators having no publication were more in ST Schools (92%) than in DIETs (83%). Simply, Teacher Educators' task was essentially teaching.
- The highest percentage of Teacher Educators (19%) presented papers in (1-5) seminars and conferences at the State level.
- At the State level, 9 percentage of Teacher Educators of DIETs presented papers in (1-3) seminars but in case of ST Schools it was only two percentage.
- As regards the **Hobbies** of the Teacher Educators, both in DIETs and ST Schools :
  - 21 percentage devoted time to reading newspapers, novels, religious books, magazines, etc.
  - 14 percentage liked to write research articles, poems, stories. one-act play.
  - Two Teacher Educators out of 241 liked to write "Braille" for blind children.
  - Four percentage Teacher Educators liked to teach in lower classes, i.e. I, II and III.
  - 13 percentage of Teacher Educators took part in broadcasting programmes through TV and Radio.
  - 15 percentage of Teacher Educators had taken to "Listening" as their hobby. They very much like to listen daily news from TV and Radio and also sweet music and film songs.
  - Seven percentage of Teacher Educators liked to do social work like medical service, sanitation work of the village, solving

problems of villagers. Only three percentage of them reported their hobby as Yoga and meditation.

- A small percentage of Teacher Educators (7%) liked to do gardening.
- Only Four percentage of Teacher Educators used to keep their hobby to visit new places. 8 percentage of Women Teacher Educators expressed "cooking" new dishes as their hobby.
- Four percentage Teacher Educators liked to organise different activities like drama, sports, picnic, annual day, seminars meetings, science exhibitions, essay writings, debate competitions, etc.
- Nine percentage of Teacher Educators were interested to play different games such as cricket, football, volleyball, etc.

(iii) Professional

- In case of DIETs, out of 135 Teacher Educators, only 28 (21%) were Senior Teacher Educators and only 06 (4%) persons were in the post of vice-principal. In case of ST Schools, all the teaching staff excepting the Headmaster or Headmistress were designated as Asst. teachers.
- As regards the experience, 52 percentage of the Teacher Educators had less than five years of teaching experience in DIETs. In case of ST Schools, it was 48 percent.
- Twenty-three percentage of Teacher Educators of DIETs had more than 11 years of experience but in case of ST Schools, it was 30 percentage. So more experienced teachers were present in ST Schools.
- About the past experience, 56 percentage of Teacher Educators of ST Schools had more than 10 years of teaching experience at the high school level. 41 percentage of Teacher Educators of DIETs

had more than 10 years of teaching experience at the high school level.

- Some Teacher Educators of DIETs (20%) also had teaching experience at the college level.
- DIETs were opened in Orissa in the year 1989, so 11 percentage of Teacher Educators of DIETs had no past experience. In other words, such Teacher Educators were inducted directly in to DIET cadre.
- There were three types of Teacher Educators in DIETs. Some of them were appointed through State Selection Board, some of them came from the defunct B.Ed Colleges, and some Senior Teacher Educators were deputed from Secondary schools.
- The promotion system for DIETs teaching staff had not been streamlined so far.
- It was observed that 36 percentage and 31 percentage of Teacher Educators of DIETs and ST Schools respectively were spending 1-3 hours per week in teaching.
- 30 percentage of Teacher Educators of DIETs and 24 percentage of ST Schools were spending 4-6 hours in teaching per week.
- Teacher Educators of ST Schools were spending more hours per week in teaching than that of DIETs.
- All the Teacher Educators of ST Schools were not trained in new specific areas like SOPT, DPEP, ECCE, NFE, etc. But in case of DIETs, all the Teacher Educators were trained in new approaches and conducting training programmes for in-service teachers.
- As high as 41 percentage of Teacher Educators of DIETs were devoting minimum 1-3 hours per week, 19% devoting 4-6 hours, 22% devoting 7-9 hours and 18% devoting 10-12 hours per week for training.
- Some of the Teacher Educators of DIETs were state level resource persons for Joyful learning and DPEP (activity based) training. So most of the

time they were engaged in imparting training in different districts.

- In ST Schools, only 12 percentage of Teacher Educators devoted 10-12 hours for conducting in-service training in different subjects like, Mathematics, MIL, Science, English and Social Studies.
- All the students both in ST Schools and DIETs had to deliver 32 lessons in different classes from I to VII, both in single classes and double classes.
- 29 percentage of Teacher Educators of ST Schools were not spending any time in practice teaching. 25% of Teacher Educators were devoting 1-3 hours, and 17% of Teacher Educators were devoting 10-12 hours to practice teaching.
- 43 percentage of Teacher Educators of DIETs were devoting 1-3 hours and 11% were devoting 10-12 hours to practice teaching.
- About one-forth of Teacher Educators of DIETs and ST Schools, i.e. 27% and 24% spent 1-3 hours per week for administration.
- As high as 50 percentage, of Teacher Educators of DIETs and only 18 percentage in ST Schools spent more time for action research work. Four percentage of research minded Teacher Educators devoted 10-13 hours per week to research work.
- The Teacher Educators of DIETs were exposed to one induction course organised by SCERT for five days in the year 2000 after 8 to 9 years of their new appointments therein.
- The SOPT programmes were organised by SCERT on Operation Black Board, Art and Aesthetic, Work-Experience and Methods of Teaching, etc. for Teacher Educators for DIETs and ST Schools.
- Similarly 33 percentage of Teacher Educators from DIETs and 28 percentage from ST Schools attended one five-days course on MLL.
- Teacher Educators participated in the workshop on preparation of the training modules in different subjects.

- Since Distance Education has assumed greater importance, various in-service education courses were organised by various agencies like SIET, DEP-DPEP, DEP-IGNOU, New-Delhi.
- Ten percentage of teacher Educators of DIETs, attended the TV and Radio programmes on Mathematics, Science and Languages.
- Teacher Educators, both from DIETs and S.T. schools were given training on methods and techniques of teaching in various subjects.
- A number of various in-service courses were organised on specific subjects like Non-formal, ECCE, Action-Research Population Education, etc.
- Majority of Teacher Educators of DIETs (47%) and (31%) of ST Schools rated their salaries as "good." But 20 percentage of Teacher Educators of DIETs and ST Schools rated their salaries as poor.
- The highest percentage of Teacher Educators of DIETs (52%) and of ST Schools (62%) rated their relation with non-teaching staff as "good."
- As high as 60 percentage of Teacher Educators of DIETs and 58 percentage in ST Schools reported the facility available for research as "poor."
- The facilities like study leave for M.Phil. or Ph.D. were not available to the Teacher Educators of DIETs and ST Schools.
- About their relation with students, none of the Teacher Educators of DIETs and ST Schools reported as "poor." The highest percentage, i.e. 78 and 57 of Teacher Educators respectively in DIETs and ST Schools responded as "good."
- Very few Teacher Educators of DIETs were the members of different Associations like Indian Association of Educational Planning and Administration, Sishuvikas Kendra, Rotary Club, Indian Association of Teacher Educators (IATE), Indian Association of Pre-school Education (IAPE), Bharat Gyan Vigyan Samiti (BGVS), All India People's Learning Research and Development, Zilla Saksharata Samiti, Sishu Sahitya Academy

and also the committee member of Board of Secondary Education, Orissa.

- As high as 33 percentage and 31 percentage of Teacher Educators of DIETs and ST Schools respectively were drawing Rs. 5000 to Rs. 6000 as their monthly salary. Only 10% Teacher Educators in ST Schools and 13% in DIETs were getting Rs. 9000 to Rs. 10000.
- Only one of the Teacher Educator of DIET, Khurda, Orissa had gone to the U.K for Non-formal education. Nobody from ST Schools had gone to any other country for academic purpose, as there was no provision for the Teacher Educators to go to aboard for professional development.
- Only 12 out of 135 Teacher Educators of DIETs took part in conducting research studies. Eight Teacher Educators published their articles in different journals and three Teacher Educators published their books in education and literature. In case of ST Schools, only four Teacher Educators wrote articles and out of them only two Teacher Educators published their articles in educational journals.

6.9.2 Opinionnaire

- As high as 80 percentage of experts opined that there should be one type of Elementary Teacher Education Institutions.
- According to them teachers trained in Teacher Education should be appointed as Teacher Educators and the Headmasters. Principals should be appointed from among the Senior Teacher Educators.
- Maximum number (90%) of experts opined that DIETs of Orissa were better equipped than the S.T. schools for importing both pre-service and in-service training.
- In most of the S.T. Schools (83%), teachers with

- Majority of the experts were of the view that adequate facilities should be provided to the Teacher Educators for conducting Action Research/Research studies and also writing articles/papers for publication in the journals.
- About the increase of participation in co-curricular activities, 53 percentage of experts opined that some weightage should be given to the interest and experience of Teacher Educators at the time of their selection.
- As high as 57 percentage of experts also suggested that the staff council meeting might be organised for identification and planning of co-curricular activities according to the resources available.
- A large percentage, i.e. 77% of the Teacher Educators having talent, experience and expertise in various co-curricular activities should be identified and assigned the responsibilities. The progress in curricular and co-curricular activities should be reviewed in the staff meetings from time to time. A large percentage, i.e. 80, opined that as the co-curricular activities have a number of advantages, the physical, mental social activities, etc. should be given due importance in the Teacher Education Programme.
- Only 40 percentage of experts suggested that the co-curricular activities like SUPW, Art and Aesthetics, Community Survey, NCC, NSS, Red-Cross should get due importance in the schedule of work.
- As high as 67 percentage of experts opined that the Teacher Educators with specialisation in respective fields were not appointed properly in DIETs, as the Teacher Educators in position had come from private training colleges, some from Secondary Schools through adjustment process and some through State Selection Board.
- According to 40 percentage of experts, the number of teaching staffs in the S.T. schools are in the range of 3 to 6 only and they had no requisite

qualification to teach Modern Science, Educational technology, Curriculum Development, etc.

- The entire 100 percentage of experts felt that the old C.T. syllabus was still continuing in DIETs and S.T. schools of Orissa and the different departments of DIET such as PSTE (Pre-Service Teacher Education), W.E. (Work Experience), DRU (District Resource Unit), IFIC (In-service Programmes, Field interaction and innovation co-ordinattion), CMDE (Curriculum, Material Development and Evaluation), E.T. (Educational Technology) were not functioning properly according to the norms of M.H.R.D. (Ministry of Human Resource Development).
- According to 37 percentage of experts, the library and laboratory of DIETs and S.T. Schools were not well equipped to meet the emerging needs of the primary syllabus.
- As high as 51 percentage of experts pointed out that the salaries of Teacher Educators were not fixed according to their educational qualification.
- About the problems of DIET, 27 percentage of experts mentioned that the main problem was the integrated staff position, the other problems were non-provision of supervision and monitoring system of training programmes, lack of proper facilities of working and service conditions and also the absence of promotional facilities for the existing staff.
- About the duration, design and content of Teacher Education programme at the elementary stage, the entire 100 percent experts opined that the duration of training should be two years and the design content should be need-based and local-specific. Physical Education, Moral Education, Yoga, value education, Art and Aesthetic Education should also be included in the syllabus.
- As regards the evaluation system, 23 percentage of experts suggested that about 60 percentage weightage should be given to the internal

assessment of skills relating to teaching, management and evaluation and on successful completion of the internal examination, a student-teacher would be allowed to appear the final examination.

- As high as 77 percentage of experts advised that evaluation should be done only by the Teacher Educators of DIETs and S.T. schools taking into consideration of their experience in teaching the particular subject instead of entrusting the work to the teachers of Secondary and Elementary schools.
- Only 33 percentage of experts opined that more emphasis should be given on the performance of the trainees in non-scholastic areas like involvement in different activities, attitude towards teaching profession, interest in co-curricular activities, etc. and grades should be awarded to the candidates on the basis of their performance.
- Suggestions were divided into two categories: (i) academic, and (ii) administrative were received from the experts for improving the existing system of Teacher Education at the Elementary level.

(i) Academic

- A high percentage (83%) of experts have observed that qualified persons should be appointed as Teacher Educators both in DIETs and S.T. Schools. Their qualification should be M.A., M.Ed. They should learn the local dialect and should like their culture with whom they have to work.
- They should be encouraged to conduct research mainly Action research. Besides, they need be exposed to various refresher courses from time to time.
- Experienced Teacher Educators might be invited to the DIETs and S.T. schools for interacting with the faculty members on the current issues and latest trends in Teacher Education.

- The Teacher Educators with the help of student-teachers should prepare TLM (teaching learning material) which will help them in transacting the curriculum.

(ii) Administrative

As high as 77 percentage of experts have given their suggestions about the administrative development. Among them, 60 percentage experts advised the Principals of DIETs need be appointed from among the experienced Senior Teacher Educators and they should be filled up from among the Teacher Educators with adequate experience.

- 43 percentage of experts suggested that the hostel facilities for girls trainees and quarters for lady teachers should be provided in S.T. Schools.
- According to 27 percentage of experts, each DIET and S.T. School should adopt some primary schools for qualitative improvement of teaching.
- About 53 percentage of experts suggested that a good rapport should be maintained with all agencies like AIR, Doordarshan and other media, C.D.P.O., Anganwadi Centres, D.Is, S.Is, C.Is, BDOs, NFE-Coordinators, VEC members, etc. for conducting in-service training programmes. Since the Zillaparishada was entrusted with the management of Elementary Education, the DIET might be treated as the advisory body and proper rapport should be maintained among them.

Advice was elicited for suggesting measures for bringing about excellence in Teacher Education programme. 100 percentage of experts responded to the question and suggestions were as follows:

- DIETs should be established in all districts of the state and uniformity in regard to course, facility, qualification and status of Teacher Educators should be maintained.
- Provision should be made for the professional

growth of the Teacher Educators such as M.Phil., Ph.D., D.Litt. by providing various facilities like study leave, advance increment, etc.

- At the national and state levels, Teacher Education Association should be organised taking the Teacher Educators of DIETs and S.T. Schools as their members, Interaction, exchange of idea, implementing innovative and relevant projects should be organised by the help of Association to promote excellence in Teacher Education.
- Various co-curricular activities should be organised to develop inter-personal and inter-cultural relationship among Teacher Educators.
- State and national workshops should be organised to promote inter-personal and inter cultural relationship among Teacher Educators.
- State and National workshops should be organised to promote professional growth of the Teacher Educators.

6.9.3 Observation Schedule

- In ST Schools, there is extremely divergent staff position. Therefore, the scenario as evident from the data gives a very sorry state of affairs.
- The qualification and experience of Headmasters of ST Schools showed lack of academic leadership.
- The selection procedure and counselling process were found defective which resulted in harassment, discriminations and extra expenditure.
- There was no minimum hostel facilities in ST Schools and DIETs.
- Centres for examination were located in distant places where even the minimum facilities of boarding and lodging were not available.
- Project work was introduced in new CT syllabus without adequate teacher in position which posed difficulty both for teachers and students.
- Supervision was not conducted systematically for years together.
- The faculty members of DIETs have come from

different branches which have led to imbalanced staff position and undesirable mismatch between the competency required, on the one hand and actual aptitude and ability of Teacher Educators on the other.

- The Heads of Training Institutions, not properly selected, were found lacking in vision and instructional leadership.

6.9.4 *Interview Schedule*

- Due to organization of many in-service training programmes at a particular period, there was heavy pressure on the staff members, causing deterioration in quality.
- In place of activity-based, participatory and interactive methodology, the delivery mechanism was found to be conventional and stereotyped.
- The audio-visual teaching aids available were not properly utilized in the training programmes.
- Both internal and external resource persons were engaged for conducting in-service training programmes but majority of them were internal faculty members.

B. RECOMMENDATIONS

On the basis of the major findings of the study, the following recommendations were made for removing the deficiencies and improving the existing status of Teacher Education at the Elementary level.

- Data showed that there was no uniformity in the recruitment of Teacher Educators of DIETs. The Teacher Educators were appointed or transferred from different fields and cadres of the Education Department. On account of this difficulty, Teacher Educators had different background and service experiences leading to want of proper vision and involvement in Teacher Education. As the Teacher

Educators of DIETs were the key persons in Elementary Teacher Education and their service conditions were different, a separate cadre should be created and recruitment rules be framed as early as possible.

- As per the Guidelines of DIET, 1989, the Teacher-Educators were to be promoted to higher positions with better pay scale after a period of 8 years of service. But even after a period of 10 years, no promotion has been given to the Teacher-Educators originally recruited for the purpose. Therefore there was lack of encouragement and motivation among Teacher Educators. Hence, the Guidelines given by Ministry of Education should be followed scrupulously in the promotion procedure.
- Due to shortage of staff members in ST Schools, Teacher Educators of ST Schools were hard-pressed and some departments of DIETs were non-functional. Hence, the existing vacancies in the ST Schools and DIETs need be filled up on priority basis.
- Only 4 percentage of Teacher Educators liked to organise different cocurricular activities like drama, sport, picnic, seminars, meetings, science-exhibitions, essay writings, debates, etc., which were believed to contribute to the professional growth of Teacher Educators. Hence, incentives and encouragement should be provided for participation of more Teacher Educators in this kind of co-curricular activities.
- Only six percent and 13 percentage of Teacher Educators of DIETs possessed Ph.D. and M.Phil. Degrees respectively, whereas no Teacher Educator of ST Schools had these qualifications. Similar was the case as regards other Post-Graduate qualifications of these Teacher Educators. Hence, necessary steps need be taken for the appointment of Teacher Educators with higher qualification not only in DIETs but also in ST Schools.

- Since 47 percentage of Teacher Educators of DIET and 23 percentage of Teacher-Educators of ST Schools possessed Masters Degree, it is desirable to appoint Teacher-Educators with Post-Graduate Degrees as per the NCTE norms.
- Although research activities are essential for professional growth of Teacher-Educators, only 10 percentage of them had Ph.D. Degrees. Hence, incentives should be provided for conducting research particularly action research in ST Schools and DIETs.
- It was found that higher percentage of Teacher Educators working in DIETs and ST schools had relative role preference and its value was found to be significant at the 0.01 level of confidence. Hence, by improving service conditions, they can have better role preference necessary for better professional growth.
- Since 33 percentage of Teacher Educators both in DIETs and ST Schools were interested both in teaching and research, they should be provided with adequate facilities for promoting both these activities for their professional growth.
- Since a small percentage (DIET-12% and STS-6%) of Teacher Educators had publications to their credit, it is better to encourage them to write articles and books for their professional growth.
- Teacher Educators may be encouraged to develop hobbies that would help their cognitive, affective and psychomotor capabilities, as the hobbies of Teacher Educators were found to be unsatisfactory (21% in reading Magazings, Papers, Books, 14% in writting research articles, 15% in listening to TV/ Redio, 8% in Cooking and 9% in Sports and Games.)
- It was found that 16% in DIET faculty and 30% in STS were devoting 10-12 hrs to teaching and one third of Teacher-Educators were found hard pressed with heavy work load. It is essential to rationalise their work load for better mental health and service conditions.

- The data showed that only for once Induction course was organised for Teacher Educators, after 10 years of their service Therefore Induction courses should be organised for Teacher Edcators at least within 3 to 6 months of their appointment, so that they could have an idea about their job-chart and nature of their duties and responsibilities.
- As it was evidenced that 100% in DIETs and 25% in STSs attended SOPT training, it is necessary that all the Teacher Educators of DIETs as well as ST Schools should be given equal opportunities for their participation in different in-service training programmes. Since Teacher Educators are required to organise different types of in-service training programmes, they need be trained in these lines earlier to gain adequate competency in implementing the programme effectively.
- It was found that a small percentage (4% to 6%) of Teacher Educators from ST Schools were provided with in-service training programmes. With a view to improving their competency, it is felt imperative to enable them to participate in the in-service training programmes conducted by various agencies.
- There were wide variations (43% in DIETs and 25% in STs devoting 1-3 hours) in organisation and supervision of practice teaching. It is necessary to encourage all of them to take responsibilities adequately for doing justice to their profession. Practices teaching may be made rigorous and stringent.
- Since it was found that 31% in DIETs and 18% in STS were devoting 1-3 hours for conducting Action Research, it is desirable that all the Teacher Educators may be encouraged to conduct Action Research and participate in research activities at the institutional level.
- With a view to giving wider exposure to the Teacher Educators through their participation in

various seminars and conferences, it is necessary to encourage the Teacher Educators for enrolling themselves as members of different associations and organisations like IAEP & A (Indian Association of Educational Planning and Administration), IAPE (Indian Association of Pre-school Education), BGVS (Bharat Gyan Vigyan Samit), IATE (Indian Association of Teacher Educators) and so on.

- According to 80% of experts, there should be one type of Teacher Education Institutions at the Elementary stage as they were required to transact the same curriculum. It is, therefore, desirable that there should not be any discrimination among the Teacher Educators.
- Since it was observed by 100% of the experts that all the depertments of DIETs were not functioning properly. Government may take immediate action for activating all of them.
- Since as high as 65% of Teacher Educators and 63% experts have asked for better facilities to conduct Action Research and publish quality papers, such incentives be provided in Training Institutes for the purpose.
- According to 37% of experts the infrastructure of DIETs and ST Schools including Library and Laboratory should be adequately developed to meet the emerging academic needs of Teacher Educators.
- As suggested by 77% of experts, the practical examination of teacher trainees should be conducted by the Teacher Educators of DIETs and ST Schools in view of their experience in the field, unlike the present system of evaluation mostly conducted by Inspectors of Schools.
- The Principals of DIETs should be appointed from among the experienced Senior Teacher Educators, as observed by 60% of experts.
- As per the Guidelines, of NCTE, DIETs should be established in all the districts of the state and

uniformity be maintained in regards to curricular facilities, qualification and service condition of Teacher-Educators.

- As per the NCTE Guidelines, innovative and development projects should be organised for promoting excellence in Teacher Education programmes at the Elementary stage.
- With a view to promoting quality of Teacher Education, State and National level workshops should be organised for improving inter-personal and inter-cultural relationship among the Teacher Educators and students of DIETs and ST Schools of Orissa.
- As suggested by 27% experts, there should be adequate supervision and monitoring of DIETs and ST Schools by Internal and External agencies from time to time for improving quality in Teacher Education.
- As observed by the investigator the Audio-Visual aids should adequately be provided and properly used in the Training Institutions.
- As per the observation data collected by the investigator. The present curricular transaction suffered from stereo-typed, traditional, irrelevant and monotonous procedures and practices.
  Hence, activity-based innovation, dynamism, flexibility, child friendliness, etc. should be adopted in the curricular transaction.
- As observed by the investigator, co-curricular activities were being organized in the Teacher Education Institutions as annual rituals without proper understanding of their worth and values: personal, social, academic and so on. Adequate time and resources are not given for proper planning, organization and evaluation of these programmes. Hence, a schedule of cocurricular activities according to available resources and local talents, should be chalked out for the entire session and adequate facilities be provided for the purpose.

- Similarly the present evaluation system was found to be rigid, close, and unscientific which need be changed for making teaching learning system more open and dynamic.
- As observed by the investigator, service conditions need be improved for providing motivation and job satisfaction. Besides, a code of Professional Ethics need be developed and introduced in the training institutions among Teacher Educators for maintaining discipline and dedication.

Appendix "A"

THE TEACHER EDUCATOR DATA FORM

To____

____

____

Dear Sir/Madam,

Under the University of Sambalpur, I have registered for the D.Litt. Degree in Education on the Topic 2—"AN ACADEMIC AND PROFESSIONAL PROFILE OF TEACHER EDUCATORS AT THE ELEMENTARY EDUCATION LEVEL.

The first step of my research work is the construction of a questionnaire under the title "Teacher Educator Data Form", which is designed in three parts to collect information relating . to demographic, academic and professional characteristics of 'Teacher Educators' of Orissa.

I earnestly request you to spare sometime out of your busy schedule to fill-in the "Teacher Educator Data Form" enclosed herewith and to please return it with your comments/suggestions to the address given below at your earliest convenience. A self-addressed stamped envelope is enclosed.

Please accept my heart-felt thanks and regards.

Your's sincerely,
Encl.: As stated above Date
(Dr. Susandhya Mohanty)
DIET, Ainthapalli,
P.O. Budharaja, Dist. 2 Sambalpur

RESPONSE INSTRUCTIONS

1. Please answer the following questions.
2. Most of the questions below can be answered by simply putting a tick mark (√) in the square which indicate what you consider the most appropriate response.
3. In some questions you are to mention your response freely.

A. DEMOGRAPHIC DATA

1. Name and Address ____________________
   ____
   ____

2. Your age: __________
3. Your Sex: Male ☐ Female ☐
4. Your Religion: __________
5. Are you a member of

   SC Yes ☐ No ☐

   ST Yes ☐ No ☐

   OBC Yes ☐ No ☐

6. Your place of Birth: Rural ☐ Urban ☐

7. Your Mother Tongue: ____________________

8. Your Health

   Excellent ☐
   Very good ☐
   Average ☐
   Somewhat poor ☐
   Poor ☐

9. Your married status:

Unmarried ☐

Married ☐

Separated ☐

Divorced ☐

B. ACADEMIC DATA

10. Please mark
A. All degrees that you have required______________________
B. (if any) degree(s) for which you are currently working

Degree	*Now held*	*Working toward*
	B.Ed.	
M.Ed.		
M.Phil.		
Ph.D./D.Phil.		
D.Litt./D.Sc.		
Other, if any (Please specify)		

11. Number of students enrolled that last year in the course(s) that you teach.

12. Do your interests lie primarily in teaching or in research?
    i. Very heavily in teaching. ☐
    ii. In both, but leaning towards teaching ☐
    iii. In both, equally ☐
    iv. In both, but leaning towards research ☐
    v. Very heavily in research ☐

13. How many scholarly books or monographs have you published or edited?

None ☐ 1-5 ☐ 6-10 ☐ Above 10 ☐

14. In about how many Seminars/Conferences have you presented paper at the State level and at the National level?

	State	*National*
None	☐	☐
1-5	☐	☐
6-10	☐	☐
11-15	☐	☐
16-20	☐	☐
Above 20	☐	☐

15. Please mention any hobby that you enjoy most.

Name of the hobby	*How long*	*Distinction/ Recognition*
____________	____________	____________
____________	____________	____________
____________	____________	____________

C. PROFESSIONAL DATA

16. What is your present rank?

Teacher	☐
Teacher Educator	☐
Senior Teacher Educator	☐
Vice-Principal	☐
Principal	☐

17. Experience as a Teacher Educator/Teacher/Lecturer

In DIET/ST School ☐ in years

In High School ☐ in years

In Colleges ☐ in years

18. During the present term, how many hours per week, are you actually spending on the following activities:

	None	1-3	4-6	7-9	10-12
A. Regular Teaching	☐	☐	☐	☐	☐
B. Conduct of Training	☐	☐	☐	☐	☐
C. Practice Teaching	☐	☐	☐	☐	☐
D. Administration	☐	☐	☐	☐	☐
E. Action research	☐	☐	☐	☐	☐

19. Please furnish the following information regarding the In-service education courses you have attended.

Name of the Programme	*Content*	*Duration*	*Organised by*	*Any follow-up*

20. How would you rate each of the following?

	Excellent	Good	Fair	Poor
A. Your own salary	☐	☐	☐	☐
B. Relationship between teaching and Non-teaching staff	☐	☐	☐	☐
C. General research facility (Library, Laboratory)	☐	☐	☐	☐
D. Availability of funds from different sources	☐	☐	☐	☐
E. Relation with students	☐	☐	☐	☐

21. In which of the committee of your Institution, you are a member

A. Admission ☐

B. Administration ☐

C. Examination ☐

D. Function ☐

E. Sports ☐

F. Magazine ☐

G. Others, if any ☐

22. Are you a member of any other faculty/body/ Association?

Yes ☐ No ☐

If yes please mention the name of the body ________

____

23. What is your gross monthly income at present?

Rs. [ ]

24. Have you ever been to a Foreign country for academic purpose?

Yes [ ] No [ ]

Where and why ____________________
____
____

25. How many research studies?

(a) Conducted ____________________
____

(b) Published ____________________
____

Thank you very much for your co-operation and fortaking the time to complete this questionnaire.

FIRST SCHEDULE TO THE NATIONAL COUNCIL FOR TEACHER EDUCATION DETERMINATION OF QUALIFICATIONS FOR RECRUITMENT OF TEACHERS IN SCHOOLS) (AMENDMENT) REGULATIONS, 2003

Recruitment qualifications for recruitment of teachers in educational institutions mentioned in Section 2 of these Regulations.

LEVEL	MINIMUM ACADEMIC AND PROFESSIONAL QUALIFICATIONS
I. Pre-School/Nursery (for children in the age group of 4-6 years)	(i) Secondary School (Class ten) certificate or its equivalent; and (ii) Diploma/Certificate in Pre-school teacher education programme of a duration of not less than one year.
II. Pre-School/Nursery followod by first two years in a formal school. Fcr children in the age-group of 4-6 and 6-8 years)	(i) Senior Secondary School (class twelve) Certificate or Intermediate or its equivalent with at least 45% marks; and (ii) Diploma/Certificate in Nursery teacher education programme of a duration of not less than two years.
III. Elementary (a) Primary	(i) Senior Secondary School certificate *or* Intermediate or its equivalent; and (ii) Diploma or certificate in basic teachers' training of a duration of not less than two years. OR Bachelor of Elementary Education (B.El.Ed.)
(b) Upper Primary (Middle school section)	(i) Senior Secondary School certificate *or* Intermediate or its equivalent; and (ii) Diploma or certificate in elementary teachers' training of a duration of not less than two years. OR Bachelor of Elementary Education (B.El.Ed.) OR Graduate with Bachelor of Education (B.Ed.) *or* its equivalent.
IV. Secondary/High Schcol	Graduate with Bachelor of Education (B.Ed.) or its equivalent. OR Four years' integrated B.Sc., B.Ed. or an equivalent course.

IV. Senior Secondary/ PUC/..............	Masters Degree in the relevant subject with Bachelor of Education (B.Ed.) its equivalent. OR Two years' integrated M.Sc.Ed. course *or* an equivalent course.

APPENDIX "B"

OPINIONNAIRE FOR EXPERTS

1. What is your opinion about the different types of Teacher Education Institutions at the Elementary state.

Yes	No

2. Is a professional degree in Education essential for the Teacher Educators ?

   Please state the reasons for either case.

3. What should be the minimum educational background of pupil teachers at the Elementary level ?

4. Please suggest improvement needed to enable Teacher Educators to contribute articles/papers on their profession.

5. How can Teacher Educators participation be increased in co-curricular activities?

Appendix "C"

AN OBSERVATION SCHEDULE FOR DOCUMENTATION OF DATA AND COLLECTION OF FEEDBACK FROM THE INSTITUTIONS

1. Name of the Teacher Educations Institution.
2. Courses Provided:

   (1)
   (2)

3. Total strength of the staff.

   (1) Sanctioned
   (2) Posted

4. Total students' strength in different courses.

5. Results of last three years (different examinations)

6. Various In-service courses — The date Started — The date Concluded

   (1)

   (2)

   (3)

7. Problems faced in:

   (1) Selection and admission of students.
   (2) Organisation of the courses.
   (3) Management of co-corricular activities.
   (4) Getting sanctions/funds.
   (5) Administration and Management.
   (6) Examination/Supervision.

8. Solutions suggested to the above problems.
   (1)
   (2)
   (3)

9. Perception of Teacher Educators/Pupil Teachers about Teacher Education for the coming decades.

10. Any innovations/good practices introduced (Title, objectives Implementation, Outcomes)

(Relevant/Supporting Reports/Materials be collected).

Signature

Appendix "D"

AN INTERVIEW SCHEDULE FOR STUDYING THE RELEVANCE AND ADEQUACY OF IN-SERVICE TRAINING COURSES FROM THE TEACHER EDUCATORS

(A) BRIEF BIO-DATA

1. Name:
2. Address:
3. Present Position:
4. Experience:
5. Qualification:

(B) ORGANISATION OF COURSES

1. Name of the courses organised
2. Duration and objectives of the course

   (a)
   (b)

3. Course content transacted (in brief)

   (a)
   (b)

4. Anything not covered during the course.

   (a)
   (b)

5. Some topics felt desirable but could not be included in the course content.

   (a)
   (b)

6. Adequacy of the duration:

   To a great extent/to some extent/not at all.

7. Resource persons *Number/Agency*

   1. Internal

   2. External

8. Methods adopted

   (a)
   (b)

9. A.V. aids utilised for Teaching Learning.

   (a)

   (b)

10. Suggestions for improving such courses.

    (a)
    (b)
    (c)

Appendix "E"

THE GAZETTE OF INDIA: EXTRAORDINARY (PART-III—SEC.-4), NCTE

Norms and Standards for Elementary Teacher Education Programme

1. Preamble

The elementary teacher education programme is meant for preparing teachers for elementary schools (Primary and upper primary/middle).

2. Duration and Intake

(a) The elementary teacher education programme shall be of a duration of two academic years.

(b) For effective curriculum transaction and for ensuring optimum utilisation of physical and instructional infrastructure and expertise of the teaching staff, there shall be a unit of 50 students for intake each year.

3. Eligibility

(a) Candidates with at least 45% marks in the senior secondary examination (+2), or its equivalent, are eligible for admission.

(b) Admission should be made either on the basis of marks obtained in the qualifying examination or in the entrance examination conducted by the State Government, as per the policy of the State Government.

(c) There shall be reservation of seats for SC/ST/OBC, Handicapped, Women, etc. as per the rules of the concerned State Government.

4. Curriculum Transaction and Requirement of Teaching Staff

(a) There should be at least 150 teaching days in a year exclusive of period of admission examination, etc. Besides, every teacher trainee shall be required to undergo internship in teaching (including practice teaching/skill development) at least for 30 days in nearby elementary schools.

(b) Apart from teaching of foundation subjects, there shall be provision for teaching of methods subjects relating to primary and upper primary curriculum, namely, Regional Language/Mother Tongue, English, Mathematics, Science and Social Studies.

(c) For a unit of 50 students or less. (with combined strength of 100 or less for the two year course), the full-time teaching faculty shall comprise of the Principal/Head and at least five lecturers. For intake of students in excess of the prescribed unit, the number of full time teachers shall be increased proportionately.

(d) Appointment of teachers should be so distributed as to ensure the required nature and level of expertise for teaching methodology courses and foundation courses.

(e) For teaching subjects such as physical education, art, work experience, music, information technology literacy, etc. Part-time instructors may be appointed.

5. Qualifications of Teaching Staff

(a) Principal Head

(i) Academic and professional qualification will be as prescribed for the post of Lecturer.

(ii) At least five years experience of teaching in elementary teacher education institutions.

(b) Lecturer
Good academic record with M.Ed./M.A. (Education) with 55% marks, preferably with specialisation in elementary education.
OR
Good Academic record with Master's Degree with 55% marks in the relevant school subject and Bachelor of Elementary Education (B.E.Ed), or B.Ed. preference with specialisation in elementary education, and with five years teaching experience in recognised elementary schools.

(c) A relaxation of 5% may be provided, from 55% to 50% of the marks, at the Masters level for SC/ST Category.

(d) Qualifications for other academic staff for teaching physical education art, work experience information technology literacy, etc. shall be as prescribed by the concerned State Government.

6. Administrative Staff

The administrative and other supporting staff may be provided as per the norms prescribed by the concerned State Government.

7. Infrastructeral Facilities

(a) There shall be provision for adequate number of classrooms, hall, laboratory space for conducting instructional activities for approved intake of students, rooms for the principal and faculty members and office for the administrative staff and a store. The size of instructional space shall not be less than 10 sq. ft. per student.

(b) There shall be a library equipped with text and reference books relating to prescribed courses of study, education encyclopedia, year books, electronic publications (CD-ROMs) and journals on teacher education and other software relevant to the elementary stage.

(c) There shall be games facilities with playground. Alternatively, the playground available with the attached school or local body may be utilized and where there is scarcity of space as in metropolitan towns/hilly regions, facilities for yoga, indoor games may be provided.

(d) To provide these facilities, the Management/ Institutions shall, at the time of making application, have in its possession adequate land/ land and building ownership basis free from all encumbrances. Government land acquired on long-term lease as per the law of the concerned State/ UT will also be considered valid for the purpose. Pending construction of permanent building in the above land, the institution may provide these facilities in suitable temporary premises up to a maximum period of 3 years, before expiry of which the institution should shift to its permanent building.

8. Instructional Facilities

(a) There shall be a multipurpose educational laboratory with psychology and science sections, and a workshop attached to it.

(i) The Science section shall have the apparatus and chemicals required to demonstrate all the experiments as per the syllabus of elementary schools.

(ii) The psychology section shall have facilities for conducting the following test: Sensory-motor, Intelligence (Performance, Verbal and Non-verbal), Aptitude, Personality and Interest Inventories including Projective it is provision for conducting simple Piagetian and Brunnerian experiments.

(b) There shall be hardware and software facilities for language learning.

(c) There shall be an Educational Technology Laboratory with hardware and software required for imparting information Technology (IT) literacy.

9. Terms and Conditions of Service of Staff

(a) The appointments shall be made on the basis of recommendations of the Selection Committee constituted as per the policy of the Central/ Concerned State Government.

(b) All appointments are to be made on full-time and regular basis.

(c) Government institutions/Government-aided institutions may make appointments on deputation or contract basis as an interim measure, in the absence of availability of suitable candidates recommended by appropriate bodies set-up by the concerned government.

(d) Appointment of part-time instructions and other staff can be made as per the norms of the concerned Government.

(e) The academic and other staff of the institution (including part-time staff) shall be paid such salary as may be prescribed by the concerned State Government from time to time.

(f) The management of the Institution shall discharge the statutory obligations relating to persons, gratuity, provident fund, etc.

(g) The age of superannuation of staff shall be determined by the policy of the concerned Government subject to maximum age not exceeding 65 years.

10. Financial Management

(a) The tuition fees and other fees shall be charged at rates as prescribed by the concerned State Government.

(b) In case of unaided institutions, there shall be an endowment fund of Rs. 5.00 Lakh to be operated jointly by the authorised representative of the management and an officer of the concerned Regional Committee, and a reserve fund equivalent to three months salary of the staff.

less experience were in position to handle science and technology apparatus and curricular programmes.

- A few experts (17%) expressed their views that different departments of DIETs as envisaged in the DIET Guidelines (1989) were not functioning properly due to slowness and slackness in Government. S.T. Schools, due to less number of teaching staff, i.e. 3 to 5, were not able to do proper justice to the transaction of curriculum.
- Some experts (34%) were of the view that all the S.T. Schools should be upgraded to DIETs of qualitative improvement of Teacher Education at the Elementary stage. The sanctioned posts both in DIETs and S.T. schools have not been filled up to do justice to the various curricular activities.
- As high as 97 percentage of experts told that a high professional degree in Education was very essential for Teacher Educators as they are to teach the subjects like advance psychology, methodology of educational research, methods of different subjects, child development, and some skills in problem-solving, motivating and controlling, which would help them in proper transaction of the subjects. .
- As high as 70 percentage of experts were of the view that the minimum educational background of pupil-teachers at the Elementary level should be 12 years of schooling but 30 percentage told that it should be a Bachelor Degree.
- About 77 percentage of experts opined that the Teacher Educators should be given orientation as to how research studies be conducted and reported properly.
- About 63 percentage of experts had also opined that academic climate should be created in the training institutions giving more weightage for publication of quality papers at the time of annual review. At the time of their promotion to higher cadre, the published papers of the Teacher Educators may be considered.

11. Relaxation in Eligibility/Duration of the Course

As in some States the duration of the elementary teacher education course is one year only and the eligibility for admission to such course is a pass in class ten, such States are given time up to the end of academic session 2004-2005 to switch over their programmes for bringing them in conformity with the NCTE Norms and Standards Meanwhile, recognition for reduced duration of the course, which shall not be less than one year and/or lower eligibility criteria, which shall not be less than one year and/or lower eligibility criteria, which shall not be less than a pass in class ten with at least 50% marks in aggregate, may be given subject to the condition that the certificate given by the State authorities in respect of such a course will be valid for employment within that State only and such courses including their duration and admission criteria are those that have been in existence in that State on the date when the NCTE Act. 1993 came into force.

Appendix "F"

LIST OF ELEMENTARY TEACHER EDUCATION INSTITUTIONS, ORISSA, 2004-05

1	2	3	4	5	6
1.	DIET, Kalahandi, Bhawanipatna-766001, Orissa.	Government	BSE	CT	50
2.	DIET, Remuna, Khirochoragopinath, Balasore-75618, Orissa.	Government	BSE	CT	50
3.	DIET, Sankara, Sundergarh-770020, Orissa.	Government	BSE	CT	50
4.	DIET, Khalikote Ganjam-761030, Orissa.	Government	BSE	CT	50
5.	DIET, Sambalpur-768004, Orissa.	Government	BSE	CT	50
6.	DIET, Khurda-752055, Orissa.	Government	BSE	CT	50
7.	DIET, Keonjhar-758001, Orissa.	Government	BSE	CT	50
8.	DIET, Jaypore, Koraput-764001, Orissa.	Government	BSE	CT	50
9.	DIET, Dolipur, Nagua, Jajpur-755019, Orissa.	Government	BSE	CT	50
10	DIET, Dhenkanal-759001, Orissa.	Government	BSE	CT	50
11.	DIET, Baripada, Mayurbhanj-757001,. Orissa.	Government	BSE	CT	50
12.	DIET, Phulbani, Tikabali-762010, Orissa..	Government	BSE	CT	50
13.	DIET, Balangir—767001, Orissa.	Government	BSE	CT	30
14.	Govt. Secondary Training School, Bhanjanagar, Ganjarn, Orissa-761126.	Government	BSE	CT	50
15.	Govt. Secondary Training School, Bargarh, Orissa-768028.	Government	BSE	CT	50
16.	Govt. Secondary Training School, Bhanjanagar, Ganjam, Orissa-761126.	Government	BSE	CT	50
17.	Govt. Secondary Training School, Paralakhemundi, Gajapati, Orissa-761200.	Government	BSE	CT	50
18.	Govt. Secondary Training School, Dharmagarh, Kalahandi, Orissa-766015	Government	BSE	CT	50
19.	Govt. Secondary Training School, Nawarangpur, Mirganguda, Orissa-761126.	Government	BSE	CT	50
20.	Govt. Secondary Training School, Polsara, Ganjam, Orissa-761105.	Government	BSE	CT	50
21.	Govt. Secondary Training School, Sonepur, Subarnapur, Orissa-767017.	Government	BSE	CT	50

22.	Govt. Secondary Training School, Kuanramunda, Sundararh, Orissa-770039.	Government	BSE	CT	50
23.	Govt. Secondary Training School, Bissam Cuttack, Ravaada, Koraput, Orissa.	Government	BSE	CT	50
24.	Govt. Secondary Training School, Nayagarh, Rajsunakhala, Orissia.	Government	BSE	CT	50
25.	Govt. Secondary Training School, Patnagarh, Bolangir, Orissa-767025.	Government	BSE	CT	50
26.	Govt. Secondary Training School, Bagudi, Balasore, Orissa-756045.	Government	BSE	CT	50
27.	Govt. Secondary Training School, Agarpara, Bhadrak, Orissa.	Government	BSE	CT	50
28.	Govt. Secondary Training School, Chhendipada, Angul, Orissa-759124.	Government	BSE	CT	50
29.	Govt. Secondary Training School, Jagatsinghpur, Orissa-754032.	Government	BSE	CT	50
30.	Govt. Secondary Training School, Pipli, Puri, Orissa-752104.	Government	BSE	CT	50
31.	Govt. Secondary Training School, Kendrapadd, Orissa-754211.	Government	BSE	CT	50
32.	Govt. Secondary Training School, Ragadi, Banki, Cuttack, Orissa-754008.	Government	BSE	CT	50
33.	Govt. Secondary Training School, Gunupur, Orissa-765022.	Government	BSE	CT	50
34.	Govt. Secondary Training School, Tangi, Khurda, Orissa-751001.	Government	BSE	CT	50
35.	Govt. Secondary Training School, (Women) Bhubaneswar, Unit-VI, Khurda, Orissa-751001.	Government	BSE	CT	50
36.	Govt. Secondary Training School, Boudh, Orissa-762014.	Government	BSE	CT	50
37.	Govt. Secondary Training School, Kishorenagar, Angul, Orissa-759122.	Government	BSE	CT	50
38.	Govt. Secondary Training School, Fakirpur, Keonjhar, Orissa-738002.	Government	BSE	CT	50
39.	Govt. Secondary Training School, Kishorenagar, Angul, Orissa-759122.	Government	BSE	CT	50
40.	Govt. Secondary Training School, Titlagarh, Balangir, Orissa-767033.	Government	BSE	CT	50
41.	Govt. Secondary Training School, Langaleswar, Balasore, Orissa.	Government	BSE	CT	50
42.	Govt. Secondary Training School, Kundukela, Sundergarh, Orissa-770019.	Government	BSE	CT	50
43.	Govt. Secondary Training School, Nimapara, Pun, Orissa-752106.	Government	BSE	CT	50
44.	Govt. Secondary Training School, Rernuli, Keonjhar, Onissa-758047.	Government	BSE	CT	50
45.	Govt. Secondary Training School, Umerkote, Nawarangapur, Orissa-764073	Government	BSE	CT	50
46.	Govt. Secondary Training School, Balia. Bhagabanpur, Kendmapama, Orissa-754234.	Government	BSE	CT	50

(Contd.)

APENDIX "F" *(Contd.)*

1	2	3	4	5	6
47.	Govt. Secondary Training School, Deogamh, Purnagarh, Orissa-768119.	Government	BSE	CT	50
48.	Govt. Secondary Training School, Pahimahura, Banikpur Bazar, Bhadrak, Orissa-756122.	Government	BSE	CT	50
49.	Govt. Secondary Training School, Puri, Orissa-7520014.	Government	BSE	CT	50
50.	Govt. Secondary Training School, Women, Berhampur, Ganjam, Orissa-760001.	Government	BSE	CT	50
51.	Govt. Secondary Training School, Nawapara, Orissa-766105.	Government	BSE	CT	50
52.	Govt. Secondary Training School, Baripada, Mayurbhanj, Orissa-757001.	Government	BSE	CT	50
53.	Govt. Secondary Training School, Gorumahisani, Mayurbhanj, Orissa-757042.	Government	BSE	CT	50
54.	Govt. Secondary Training School, Kusalda, Mayurbhanj, Orissa-757085.	Government	BSE	CT	50
55.	Govt. Secondary Training School, (Urdu), Shaikh Bazar, Tulasipur, Cuttack, Orissa-766015.	Government	BSE	CT	50
56.	Govt. Secondary Training School., Tudigadia, Sore, Balasore, Orissa-756045.	Government	BSE	CT	50
57.	Govt. Secondaiy Training School, Chandini Chowk, Cuttack, Orissa-753002.	Government	BSE	CT	50
58.	Govt. Secondary Training School, Bhalulata, Sundergarh, Orissa.	Government	BSE	CT	50
59.	Govt. Secondary Training School, Bolangir, Orissa-767001.	Government	BSE	CT	50
60.	Govt. Secondary Training School, Athagarh, Cuttack, Orissa-754001	Government	BSE	CT	50
61.	Govt. Secondary Training School, Chitrakonda, Malkanagiri, Orissa-764052.	Government	BSE	CT	50
62.	Govt. Secondary Training School, Chikiti, Ganjam-7761010, Orissa	Government	BSE	CT	50
63.	Govt. Secondary Training School, Narshingpur, Cuttack, Orissa.	Government	BSE	CT	50
64.	Govt. Secondary Training School, Madhusudan Road, GPO, Buxi-Bazzar, Cuttack, Orissa-753030.	Government	BSE	CT	50
65.	Govt. Secondary Training School, Bankoi, Khurda, Orissa.	Government	BSE	CT	50

Bibliography

Adval, S.B.: *Quality of Teachers,* Amitabh Prakashan, 3, Bank Road, Allahabad, 1979.

Agarwal, J.C.: *The Progress of Education in free India,* Agya Book Depot, 30, Naiwala, Karol Bagh, New Delhi-110005, 1987.

Agarwal, J.C., and Agarwal, S.P.: *Role of Unesco in Education,* Vikas Publishing House Pvt. Ltd., Regd. Office: 5 Ansari Road, New Delhi-110002, 1982.

Agarwal, J.C. and Agarwal, S.P.: *Educational Planning in India,* Concept Publishing Company, A/15-16, Commercial Block, Mohan Garden, New Delhi-110059 (India), 1992.

Agarwal, J.C. and Biswas, A.: *Encyclopedic Dictionary and Directory of Education,* Vol. I, The Academic Publishers (India), New Delhi, 1971.

Anastasi, A.: *Psychological Testing,* MacMillan Co. Ltd., London, 1966.

Asher, William: *Educational Research and Evaluation Methods,* Waltham, M.A. Little Brown, 1976.

Basu, B.D.: *History of Education in India,* Cosmo-Publications, 24-B, Absari Road, Darya Ganj, New Delhi, 1989, p. 152.

Best, J.W.: *Research in Education,* Prentice Hall of India, New Delhi, 1978.

Best, J.W. and Khan, J.V.: *Research in Education,* Prentice Hall of India, New Delhi, 1992.

Best, J.W.: *Research in Education,* Prentice Hall of India, Private Limited, M-97, Connaught Circus, New Delhi-110001, 1983.

Board of Secondary Education: *Courses of Studies for C.T. Examination,* Cuttack, B.S.E., Orissa, 1982.

Board of Secondary Education: *Courses of Studies for Secondary Teachers, Certificates Examination,* B.S.E., Orissa, Cuttack, 2001.

Borg, W.R. and Gall, M.D.: *Educational Research—An Introduction,* New York, 1983.

Buch, M.B.: *1st Survey of Research in Education,* Head Centre of Advanced Study in Education, M.S. University of Baroda, 1974.

Buch, M.B.: *2nd. Survey of Research in Education,* Board Society for Educational Research and Development, 1979.

Buch, M.B. (Ed.): *3rd Survey of Research in Education,* NCERT, New Delhi, 1987.

Buch, M.B. (Ed.): *4th Survey of Research in Education,* New Delhi, NCERT, 1991.

Buch, M.B. (Ed.): *5th Survey of Educational Research,* NCERT 1997.

Chakrabarti, M.: *Challenges in Teacher Education,* Daya Publishing House, 74, Deva Ram Park, Trinagar, Delhi-110035, 1993.

Cron Back, L.J.: *Essentials of Psychological Testing,* Harper and Brothers, New York, 1949.

Dikshit, S.S.: *Teacher Education in Modern Democracies,* Sterling Publisher (P) Ltd., Jullundur, Delhi-6, First Edition, 1969.

Dooros, Sidney: *Teaching as a Profession,* Columbus, Ohio, Charles and Merrill, 1968.

Eby, Frederich : *The Development of Modern Education, in Theory, Organisation and Practice,* New York, Prentice-Hall, Inc. 1952.

Ed. CIL: *Programme for Improvement of Secondary Teacher Education Institutions,* (Salient Features and Guidelines for Project Formulation) A Government of India Enterprise, A 1/111, Safdarjang Enclave, New Delhi-110029, 1887.

Garrett, H.E.: *Statistics in Psychology and Education,* Langmans Greentt Co., New York, 1966.

Gimeno, Joseblat and Ibanez: *The Education of Primary and Secondary School Teachers,* the United Nations Educational, Scientific & Cultural Ricardo Marin Organisation, 7, Place De Fontenoy-75700, Paris, 1981.

Ginsburg, Mark-B: *Contradictions in Teacher Education and Society,* The Falmer Press, Taylor & Fruncis Inc., 242, Cherry Street, Philadelphia, PA 19106-1906, USA, 1988.

Good, C.V., Barr, A.S. and Scates, D.E.: *Methodology of Educational Research,* Mapleton Century Craft, New York, 1941.

Govt. of India: *Report of Indian Education Commission,* Ministry of Education and Youth Services, New Delhi, 1966.

Govt. of India: *Report of the Review Committee on the Curriculum for Ten-year School,* New Delhi, 1977.

Govt. of India: *Report of Rodhakrishnan Commission, Ministry of Education,* New Delhi, 1948, p. 3.

Govt. of India: *Report of National Commission on Teachers: The Teacher and Society,* 1983, p. 53.

Govt. of India: *District Institute of Education and Training Guidelines,* Ministry of Human Resource Development, New Delhi, 1989.

Govt. of India: *Towards an Enlightened and Human Society,* Ministry of Human Resource Development, NPE-86-A, Review, New Delhi, 1990.

Govt. of India: *Minimum Levels of Learning at Primary Stage,* Ministry of Human Resource Development, New Delhi, NCERT, 1991.

Govt. of India: *National Policy on Education, 1986,* Ministry of Human Resource Development, New Delhi, 1992.

Govt. of India: *National Policy on Education: Programme of Action (Revised),* Ministry of Human Resource Development, New Delhi, 1992.

Govt. of India: *85 year Plan 1992-97,* Vols. I & II, Planning Commission, New Delhi, 1992.

Govt. of Orissa: Report on the Activities of the School and Mass Education Department for the year, 1997-98, 1998-99, 1999-2000, 2000-2001, 2003-2004. Text Book Press, Bhubaneswar.

Govt. of Orissa: Teacher Education in Orissa, Directorate of Teacher Education and SCERT, Orissa, Bhubaneswar-2000-2001.

Goyal, J.C.: *The Indian Teacher Educator—Some Characteristics,* National Psychological Corporation 4/230, Kacheri Ghat, Agra-282004 (U.P.), India, 1985.

Goyal, J.C. and Chopra, R.K.: *The Elementary School Teacher—A Profile,* NCERT, New Delhi, 1990, p, 2.

Gupta, Arun K. and Srinivasan, Nalini: *Psycho-social and Academic Profile of Female Teacher Trainees,* Indian Education Review, Vol. 25(1), 117-23, 1990.

Hilliard, Frederich Hadawa: *Teaching the Teacher, Trends in Teacher Educational,* London, George Allen and Unwin, 1971, p. 33.

Jangira, N.K.: *Teacher Training and Teacher Effectiveness,* National Publishing House, 23, Darya Ganj, New Delhi-110002 (India), 1979, p. 1.

Joshi, K.L.: *Problems of Higher Education in India,* Popular Prakasan, Bombay, 1976.

Joshi, Rajni: *Conceptual Understanding of Professional Accountability of Teacher Educators,* M.Phil. Edu., University of Delhi, 1991.

Kaul, J.N. (Ed.): *Higher Education, Social Change and National Development,* Indian Institute of Advanced Study, Simla, 1975.

Kohil, V.K.: *Teacher Education in India,* Vivek Publishers, 285, Ram Nagar, Ambala City (India), 1992, pp. 24, 48.

Koul, L.: *Methodology of Educational Research,* Vakas Publishing House Pvt. Ltd., New Dehli, 1993.

Kundu, C.L. (Ed.): *Indian Year Book on Teacher Education,* Sterling, New Delhi, 1988, pp. 33, 370.

Lulla, B.P., Murty, S.K. and Taneja, V.B.: *Essentials of Educational Research,* N.D. Pahuja, Mohindra Capital Publishers, Chandigarh-160017.

Malhotra, R.N. and Katiyar, S.N.: *Education of Teachers in India,* Vol. I, S. Chand & Co., New Dehli, 1968.

Merelman, T.M.: *Political Socialization and Educational Climates,* Holt, Rinehart and Winston, Inc., New York, 1971.

Merriman, P.L.: *The New Dictionary of Psychology,* The Philosophical Library, Inc., New York, 1947, p. 269.

Meyer, Adolph Erich: *The Development of Education in the Twentieth Century,* Asia Publishing House, Bombay, 1960.

Mishra, A.N.: *A Study of the Teacher Education Programme at the Primary Level,* Unpublished Doctoral Dissertation, Utkal University, Bhubaneswar, Orissa, 1989.

Mohanty, J.: *Current Trends in Higher Education,* Deep & Deep Publications, F-159, Rajouri Gardern, New Delhi, 2000.

Mohanty, J.: *Human Rights Education,* Deep & Deep Publications, New Delhi, 2000.

Mohanty, J., Parida, K.K. and Choudhury, S.K.: *Principles of Education and School Organisation,* Takshasila, Cuttack, 1998.

Mohanty, J.: *Child Development & Education Today,* Deep & Deep Publication, New Delhi, 1998.

Mohanty, J.: *Educational Administration, Management, Planning, Inspectionand School Organisation.* Maneka Prakashan, Sambalpur, 1996.

Mohanty, J. and Nanda, B.K.: *Modern Trends & Issues in Education,* Takshasila, Cuttack, 1996.

Mohanty, J.: *Dynamics of Higher Education,* Deep & Deep Publications, New Delhi, 1994.

Mohanty, J.: *Foundation of Education,* Takshasila, Cuttack, 1994.

Mohanty, J.: *Teacher & Education in the Emerging Society,* Takshasila, Cuttack, 1993.

Mohanty, J.: *Current issues in Education,* Cosmo Publications, 24-B, Ansari Road, Darya Ganj, New Delhi, 1992.

Mohanty, J.: *Adult and Non-formal Education,* Deep & Deep Publication, New Delhi, 1992.

Mohanty, J.: *Educational Administration, Supervision & School Management,* Deep & Deep Publications, New Delhi, 1992.

Mohanty, J.: *Educational Administration, Supervision & Finance,* Takshasila, Cuttack, 1991.

Mohanty, J.: *Modern Trends in Indian Education,* Takshasila, Cuttack, 1990.

Mohanty, J.: *Democracy and Education in India,* Deep & Deep Publication, New Delhi, 1988.

Mohanty, J.: *Education in India: Impact of Education,* Deep & Deep Publications, New Delhi, 1988.

Mohanty, J.: Development of Teacher Education in Orissa, A comprehensive and critical study for meeting the challenges of the twenty-first century, A project report submitted to UGC, New Delhi, under Emeritus fellowship, 2000-02.

Mohanty, J.: Teacher Education, Deep and Deep Publications Pvt. Ltd., F-159, Rajouri Garden, New Delhi-110027, 2003.

Mohd., Akhtar Siddiqui: *In-service Teacher Education,* Ashish Publishing House, 8/81, Punjabi Bagh, New Delhi-110026, 1991, p. 32.

Mouly, G.J.: *The Science of Educational Research,* Eurasia Publishing House (Pvt.) Ltd., New Delhi, 1964.

Mudaliar, A.L.: *Report of the Secondary Education Commission,* Govt. of India, New Delhi, 1953.

Mukerji, S.N.: *Education of Teachers in India,* Vol. II, S. Chand & Co., Ram Nagar, New Dehli, 1968.

NCERT: *Teacher Education Curriculum—A Framework,* New Delhi, NCERT, 1976.

NCERT: *Elementary Teacher Education Curriculum, Guidelines and Syllabi,* New Dehi, NCERT, 1991.

NCTE: *Quality Concerns in Secondary Teacher Education,* C-2/ 10, Safdarjung Development Area, Sri Aurobindo Marg, New Delhi-110016, 1998.

NCTE: *Competency-based and Commitment-oriented Teacher Education for Quality School Education (In-service Education),* C-2/10, Safdarjung Development Area, Sri Aurobindo Marg, New Delhi-110016, 1998.

NCTE: *Curriculum Framework for Quality Teacher Education,* C-2/10, Safdarjung Development Area, Sri Aurobindo Marg, New Delhi-110016, 1998.

NCTE: *NCTE Initiatives for Quality Improvement in Teacher Education Programmes,* 2001.

NCTE: *Competency-based and Commitment-oriented Teacher*

Education for Quality School Education, (Initiation Document), C-2/10, Safdarjung Development Area, Sri Aurobindo Marg, New Delhi-110016, 1998.

NCTE: *Policy Perspectives in Teacher Education,* 16, Mahatma Gandhi Marg, I.P. Estate, New Delhi-110002, 1995.

NCTE: *Different modes of Education used for Teacher Preparation in India—A Study,* 16, Mahatma Gandhi Marg, I.P. Estate, New Delhi-110002, 1995.

NCTE: Profile of Teacher Educators, Member Secretary, NCTE, C-2/10, Safdarjung Development Area, Sri Aurobindo Marg, New Delhi-110016, 1999.

Rao, D.B.: *Teacher Education in India,* Discovery Publishing House, 4831/24, Ansari Road, Prahlad Street, Durya Gunj, New Delhi, 1998.

Ross, C.C. and Stanley, J.C.: *Mesurement in Today's School,* Prentice Hall, Inc., 76, Fifth Avenue, New York, 2nd Printing, 1955.

Sanhar, Uday: *Education of Indian Teachers,* Sterling: New Delhi, 1984.

Sayed, Narullah and Naik, J.P.: *History of Education in India,* Bombay, J.H. Collins for MacMillan and Co., 1951.

Sharma, R.D. and Budhori, K.B.: *Student Teachers, Teaching Profession & Manpower Planning,* Indian Educational Review, Vol. 26(1), pp. 21-25.

Sharma, M.L.: *Educating the Educator,* The Associated Publishers, 2960, Kacha Bazar, Post Box No. 56, Ambala Cantt, India, 1988.

Sharma, S.R.: *Teacher Education in India,* Anmol Publications, 4378/417, Ansari Road, Darya Ganj, New Delhi-110002, 1992.

Sharma, Indra and Sharma, M.R.: *History and Problems of India Education, Questions and Answers,* Agra, Vinod Pustak Mandir, 1985.

Singh, L.C.: *Teacher Education in India: A Resource Book,* New Delhi, NCERT, 1990.

Singh, Nagendra: *Modernisation of Teacher Education,* Common Wealth Publishers 4378/413, Gali Muralilal, Ansari Road, Darya Ganj, New Delhi-110002, 1988.

Singh, P.: *An Evaluation Study of Teacher Education in Bihar*, Patna University, 1982.

Singh, R.P.: *The Indian Teacher*, National Publishing House, New Delhi, 1969.

Singh, R.P.: *The Challenges of Tomorrow*, Sterling Puhlishers Private Limited, L-10, Green Park, Extension, New Delhi-110016, 1993.

Sprinj Hall, C.: *Understanding Educational Research*, Prentice Hall, New Delhi, 1991.

Srivastava, R.C.: *Teacher Education in India*, Regency Publications, 20/36-G, Old Market, West Patel Nagar, New Delhi-110008, 1997, pp. 1, 36, 37.

Terry Page, G. and Thomas, J.B. with Marshall, A.R.: *International Dictionary of Education*, Printed in Great Britain by Billing & Sons Ltd., Guildford, London & Worcester, 1979.

Torsten, Husen and T. Neville Postlethwaite: *The International Encyclopedia of Education*, Vol. 7, Pergamon Press, Oxford, New York, Beijing, Frankfurt, Sao Paulo, Sydney, Tokyo, Toronto, 1988.

Vaidya, N.: *Some Reflections on Teacher Education*, Extension Services Department, NCERT, Regional College of Education, NCERT, Ajmer, Rajasthan, 1984, p. 2.

Vandalen, B.: *Understanding Educational Research, An Introduction*, McGraw-Hill, Berkeley, 1965.

Wiersma, W.: *Research Methods in Education*, Allyn and Bacon, Inc., Boston, London, 1986.

Wilson, R.C. and Gaff, J.G.: *College Professors and their Impact on Students*, John Wilerf & Sons, New York, 1975.

Index

Hence, the Opinionnaire has the following characteristics:

(i) It makes use of statement of questions on different aspects of the problem under investigation.

(ii) It solicited responses either a three point scale or five point scale.

The investigator, therefore, decided to elicit the views of the experts and veteran educationists on different aspects and factors of Teacher Education.

Taking into consideration the major components of an educational system, the Investigator developed a structured Opinionnaire to take the opinion of the experts in Education, regarding the status, present position and problems of Elementary Teacher Education Institutions. They are also requested to give advice for the qualitative improvement of Teacher Education in the state.

The Opinionnaire was individually administered by the Investigator on the personnel associated with the Elementary Teacher Education Programme at different levels. The schedule contains items on, (i) Present status of DIETs and ST schools, (ii) requirement of professional degree for Teacher Educators, (iii) minimum entry qualification required for the pupil-teachers for Elementary Teacher, (iv) how to increase interest of Teacher Educators to participate in co-curricular activities, (v) how to motivate them to contribute papers, articles in their professional [illegible], (vi) about the academic, administrative and financial problems, (vii) about the [illegible], duration and contents of Elementary Teacher Education, (viii) development of evaluation system, and (ix) suggestions about the improvement of Teacher Education at the Elementary Level. The Opinionnaire was prepared in consultation with a group of Experts in Education.

4.7.4 Observation Schedule

This tool was meant for documentation of data and collection of feedback from the Teacher Education Institutions (DIETs and ST schools). The Investigator has sought to collect data from DIETs and ST Schools through her on-the-spot